Ninja Foodi 2-Basket

Air Fryer Cookbook

Quick and Easy Recipes to Air Fry, Air Broil, Roast, Bake and Dehydrate, Incl. Tips and Tricks to Master Ninja 2 Basket Air Fryer (Color Edition)

Sophia Garlet

Legal & Disclaimer

The content and information in this book is consistent and truthful, and it has been provided for informational, educational and business purposes only.

The illustrations in the book are from the website shutterstock. com, depositphoto.com and freepik.com and have been authorized.

The content and information contained in this book has been compiled from reliable sources, which are accurate based on the knowledge, belief, expertise and information of the Author. The author cannot be held liable for any omissions and/or errors.

Table of Content

INTRODUCTION

Hello there! I'm Sophia Garlet, and let me start by saying - cooking has always been my passion. From the sizzling aromas of roasting meats to the delicate balance of flavors in a well-prepared dessert, I've found sheer joy in the kitchen.

My journey with cooking has been a delightful exploration, one that's now taken an exciting turn with the discovery of the Ninja Foodi 2-Basket Air Fryer. This ingenious appliance isn't just another kitchen gadget; it's a game-changer. Imagine the convenience of cooking two different dishes simultaneously - this feature alone has revolutionized my culinary adventures, making meal prep quicker, easier, and oh-so-efficient.

So, why am I venturing into writing a recipe book centered around this marvel? Well, it's simple. I want to share the sheer delight and ease this air fryer brings to the kitchen. This book isn't just about recipes; it's a guide that bridges the gap between novices and seasoned cooks, offering detailed steps and vibrant, mouthwatering images to inspire your culinary creativity.

Inside, you'll find a treasure trove of recipes - hearty roasted meats that practically melt in your mouth, flavorful meals marrying mains and sides seamlessly, crispy snacks that redefine "snack time," and decadent desserts that'll make every occasion a celebration. Each recipe is crafted with precision, ensuring it's as delightful to cook as it is to devour.

The Ninja Foodi 2-Basket Air Fryer isn't just a kitchen appliance; it's a culinary wizard that simplifies cooking without compromising taste or variety. And this book? It's your key to unlocking the full potential of this fantastic tool. Whether you're just starting your cooking journey or you're a seasoned chef looking for new tricks, this book has something special for you.

So, join me in this flavorful journey! Let's uncover the magic of the Ninja Foodi 2-Basket Air Fryer together. With this book in hand, you'll be mastering delightful meals in no time. It's time to elevate your cooking game - grab a copy and let's embark on this delicious adventure!

Advantages of Ninja Foodi 2-Basket Air Fryer

The Ninja Foodi 2-Basket Air Fryer boasts several advantages that make it a standout kitchen appliance:

- **Dual-Zone Cooking:** The ability to cook two different foods simultaneously saves time and effort, making meal preparation incredibly efficient.

- **Versatility:** With six cooking functions - air frying, air broiling, roasting, baking, reheating, and dehydrating - it's a multi-functional powerhouse suitable for a wide range of recipes and cooking styles.

- **XL Capacity:** The generous 8-quart capacity allows for cooking mains and sides together or preparing larger batches of food, accommodating family-sized meals.

- **Separate Heating Zones:** Each of the two 4-quart zones has its own cooking basket, cyclonic fan, and rapid heater, ensuring consistent cooking for both dishes.

- **Easy Cleaning:** Dishwasher-safe baskets and crisper plates simplify cleanup, reducing the hassle after cooking.

- **Healthier Cooking:** Its air frying technology cooks with up to 75% less fat compared to traditional deep frying methods, providing healthier yet still delicious results.

- **Wide Temperature Range:** Ranging from 105°F to 450°F, this appliance offers precise temperature control, allowing for gentle dehydration or quick crisping and cooking with convection heat.

- **Smart Finish & Match Cook Features:** The Smart Finish option synchronizes cooking times, while the Match Cook button replicates settings across zones, making it easy to manage multiple dishes simultaneously.

- **User-Friendly Controls:** Intuitive operating buttons and clear indicators simplify the cooking process, enhancing user experience for both beginners and experienced cooks.

Overall, the Ninja Foodi 2-Basket Air Fryer combines innovation, convenience, and versatility, making it a fantastic addition to any kitchen for those seeking efficient and flavorful cooking experiences.

Control Panel

The control panel of the Ninja Foodi 2-Basket Air Fryer consists of several function buttons and operating buttons to manage the cooking process effectively:

Function Buttons:

- **AIR BROIL:** This function adds a crispy finishing touch to meals or melts toppings for a perfect finish.

- **AIR FRY:** Used to achieve crispy and crunchy results with little to no oil.

- **ROAST:** Functions as a roaster oven, ideal for cooking tender meats and more.

- **REHEAT:** Warms up leftovers while retaining a crispy texture.

- **DEHYDRATE:** Allows for dehydrating meats, fruits, and vegetables to create healthy snacks.

- **BAKE:** Used to create decadent baked treats and desserts.

Operating Buttons:

- **Zone Controls:** Two sets of controls (1 and 2) manage the output for each respective basket, allowing independent temperature and time adjustments.

- **TEMP Arrows:** Up and down arrows to adjust the cooking temperature before or during the cooking cycle.

- **TIME Arrows:** Up and down arrows to adjust the cooking time in any function before or during the cook cycle.

- **SMART FINISH Button:** Automatically syncs the cook times to ensure both zones finish cooking simultaneously, even if the items have different cook times.

- **MATCH COOK Button:** Automatically matches Zone 2 settings to those of Zone 1, useful for cooking larger amounts of the same food or different foods using the same function, temperature, and time.

- **START/PAUSE Button:** Initiates cooking after selecting temperature and time. Press again to pause cooking, allowing adjustments if needed.

- **POWER Button:** Turns the unit on and off, stopping all cooking functions.

- **Standby Mode:** After 10 minutes of no interaction, the unit enters standby mode, indicated by a dimly lit Power button.

- **Hold Mode:** Appears during SMART FINISH mode, with one zone cooking while the other holds until the times sync together.

This comprehensive control panel allows for precise control over cooking temperatures, times, and functions, ensuring a seamless cooking experience with the Ninja Foodi 2-Basket Air Fryer.

How to Use the Ninja Foodi 2-Basket Air Fryer

Discovering how to maximize the Ninja Foodi 2-Basket Air Fryer is the key to effortless and versatile cooking. This guide will walk you through using the air fryer step-by-step, making meal prep a simple and enjoyable experience. Let's delve into the specifics of using this incredible appliance to create mouthwatering dishes and snacks!

1. Preparing the Air Fryer:
Place the Ninja Foodi 2-Basket Air Fryer on a flat, heat-resistant surface and ensure proper ventilation around the appliance.
Before using it for the first time, wash the baskets and crisper plates either by hand or in the dishwasher. Dry them thoroughly before use.

2. Powering On:
Press the Power button to turn on the air fryer. The Power button will light up, indicating that the unit is ready for use.

3. Selecting Cooking Functions:
Use the function buttons (AIR BROIL, AIR FRY, ROAST, REHEAT, DEHYDRATE, BAKE) to choose the desired cooking method for your recipe.

4. Adjusting Temperature and Time:
Use the TEMP arrows to adjust the cooking temperature within the recommended range for your chosen function.

Use the TIME arrows to set the cooking time required for your recipe.

5. Loading the Baskets:
Place the food items to be cooked in the designated baskets, ensuring that they are evenly distributed for efficient cooking.
For simultaneous cooking of two different foods, use the separate baskets in each zone.

6. Initiating Cooking:
Press the appropriate Zone Control button (1 or 2) to begin the cooking process for each basket. The air fryer will start operating based on the selected settings.

7. Smart Finish and Match Cook Features:
Utilize the Smart Finish button to sync cook times for both zones, ensuring that both foods finish cooking simultaneously, even if they have different cook times.
The Match Cook button replicates Zone 1 settings for Zone 2, helpful for cooking larger quantities of the same food or different foods using the same settings.

8. Monitoring and Adjusting:
During the cooking process, monitor the progress through the clear view window on the air fryer.
If needed, you can adjust the temperature or time using the TEMP and TIME arrows while the cooking cycle is in progress.

9. Pausing or Stopping Cooking:
Press the START/PAUSE button to pause the cooking process. Make necessary adjustments or checks before resuming by pressing the button again.

10. Completion and Serving:

When the cooking cycle ends, carefully remove the baskets using oven mitts or grips as they might be hot. Plate and serve your cooked food, and remember to turn off the air fryer by pressing the Power button once you're done.

Following these steps will help you effectively use the Ninja Foodi 2-Basket Air Fryer to prepare a variety of delicious dishes with ease. Always refer to the user manual and specific recipe instructions for best results.

Congratulations on navigating the depths of the Ninja Foodi 2-Basket Air Fryer! By diving into its functionalities, you've unlocked a realm of culinary efficiency. Armed with this understanding, your kitchen endeavors are set to soar. The ability to simultaneously cook two distinct dishes or whip up crispy snacks with minimal effort now lies within your grasp. Embrace this kitchen wizardry, and may each meal prepared with this appliance be a testament to your newfound culinary prowess.

As you venture forth, armed with the skills to wield this innovative tool, let your creativity flourish. Experiment with recipes, delight in the simplicity of meal preparation, and relish the joy of savoring homemade dishes that this air fryer effortlessly brings to life. Here's to many more delicious moments and effortless cooking experiences ahead!

CHAPTER 1
Breakfast

Simple Cinnamon Toasts

|PREP TIME: 5 minutes
|COOK TIME: 6 minutes

1 tbsp. salted butter
2 tsps. ground cinnamon
4 tbsps. sugar
½ tsp. vanilla extract
10 bread slices

1. In a bowl, combine the butter, cinnamon, sugar, and vanilla extract. Spread onto the slices of bread.
2. Install a crisper plate in both baskets. Place 5 bread slices in each basket.
3. Select Zone 1, select BAKE, set temperature to 380°F, and set time to 6 minutes. Select MATCH COOK to match Zone 2 settings to Zone 1. Select START/PAUSE to begin cooking, until golden brown.
4. Serve warm.

Classic Buttermilk Biscuits

|PREP TIME: 5 minutes
|COOK TIME: 7 minutes

2 cups all-purpose flour, plus more for dusting the work surface
1 tbsp. baking powder
¼ tsp. baking soda
2 tsps. sugar
1 tsp. salt
6 tbsps. cold unsalted butter, cut into 1-tbsp. slices
¾ cup buttermilk

1. In a large mixing bowl, combine the flour, baking powder, baking soda, sugar, and salt and mix well.
2. Using a fork, cut in the butter until the mixture resembles coarse meal.
3. Add the buttermilk and mix until smooth.
4. Dust more flour on a clean work surface. Turn the dough out onto the work surface and roll it out until it is about ½ inch thick.
5. Using a 2-inch biscuit cutter, cut out the biscuits.
6. Install a crisper plate in both baskets and spray with olive oil. Place half of the biscuits in a single layer in each basket.
7. Select Zone 1, select BAKE, set temperature to 360°F, and set time to 7 minutes. Select MATCH COOK to match Zone 2 settings to Zone 1. Select START/PAUSE to begin cooking.
8. When cooking is complete, serve warm.

Easy Sausage Pizza

|PREP TIME: 10 minutes
|COOK TIME: 6 minutes

2 tbsps. ketchup
1 pita bread
⅓ cup sausage
½ pound (227 g) Mozzarella cheese
1 tsp. garlic powder
1 tbsp. olive oil

1. Spread the ketchup over the pita bread.
2. Top with the sausage and cheese. Sprinkle with the garlic powder and olive oil.
3. Install a crisper plate in a basket. Place pizza in the basket, then insert basket in unit.
4. Select Zone 1, select BAKE, set temperature to 340°F, and set time to 6 minutes. Press the START/PAUSE button to begin cooking.
5. When cooking is complete, remove basket from unit. Serve warm.

Spinach Omelet

|PREP TIME: 10 minutes
|COOK TIME: 10 minutes

1 tsp. olive oil
3 eggs
Salt and ground black pepper, to taste
1 tbsp. ricotta cheese
¼ cup chopped spinach
1 tbsp. chopped parsley

1. Grease a 7 x 5-inch baking dish with olive oil.
2. In a bowl, beat the eggs with a fork and sprinkle salt and pepper.
3. Add the ricotta, spinach, and parsley. Transfer the mixture into the baking dish.
4. Install a crisper plate in a basket. Place baking dish in the basket, then insert basket in unit.
5. Select Zone 1, select AIR FRY, set temperature to 330°F, and set time to 10 minutes. Press the START/PAUSE button to begin cooking, until the egg is set.
6. Serve warm.

Apple and Walnut Muffins

|PREP TIME: 15 minutes
|COOK TIME: 10 minutes

1 cup flour
⅓ cup sugar
1 tsp. baking powder
¼ tsp. baking soda
¼ tsp. salt
1 tsp. cinnamon
¼ tsp. ginger
¼ tsp. nutmeg

1 egg
2 tbsps. pancake syrup, plus 2 tsps.
2 tbsps. melted butter, plus 2 tsps.
¾ cup unsweetened applesauce
½ tsp. vanilla extract
¼ cup chopped walnuts
¼ cup diced apple

1. In a large bowl, stir together the flour, sugar, baking powder, baking soda, salt, cinnamon, ginger, and nutmeg.
2. In a small bowl, beat egg until frothy. Add syrup, butter, applesauce, and vanilla and mix well.
3. Pour egg mixture into dry ingredients and stir just until moistened.
4. Gently stir in nuts and diced apple.
5. Divide batter among 8 parchment-paper-lined muffin cups.
6. Install a crisper plate in both baskets. Place 4 muffin cups in each basket.
7. Select Zone 1, select BAKE, set temperature to 330°F, and set time to 10 minutes. Select MATCH COOK to match Zone 2 settings to Zone 1. Select START/PAUSE to begin cooking, until toothpick inserted in center comes out clean.
8. Serve warm.

Mustard Meatballs

|PREP TIME: 15 minutes
|COOK TIME: 15 minutes

½ pound ground pork
1 onion, chopped
2 tbsps. fresh basil, chopped
½ tbsp. cheddar cheese, grated
½ tbsp. Parmesan cheese, grated
1 tsp. garlic paste
1 tsp. mustard
1 tsp. honey
Salt and black pepper, to taste

1. Mix together all the ingredients in a bowl until well combined.
2. Make small equal-sized balls from the mixture.
3. Install a crisper plate in a basket. Place meatballs in the basket, then insert basket in unit.
4. Select Zone 1, select AIR FRY, set temperature to 390°F, and set time to 15 minutes. Press the START/PAUSE button to begin cooking.
5. With 8 minutes remaining, press START/PAUSE to pause the unit. Remove the basket from unit and flip the meatballs over. Reinsert basket in unit and press START/PAUSE to resume cooking.
6. When cooking is complete, remove basket from unit. Transfer meatballs to a plate. Serve warm.

Spanish Style Frittata

Serves: 2

|PREP TIME: 10 minutes
|COOK TIME: 14 minutes

½ cup frozen corn
½ of chorizo sausage, sliced
1 potato, boiled, peeled and cubed
2 tbsps. feta cheese, crumbled
3 jumbo eggs
1 tbsp. olive oil
Salt and black pepper, to taste

1. Grease a 7 x 5-inch baking pan with olive oil.
2. Add chorizo sausage, corn and potato in the pan.
3. Install a crisper plate in a basket. Place the pan in the basket, then insert basket in unit.
4. Select Zone 1, select BAKE, set temperature to 355°F, and set time to 14 minutes. Press the START/PAUSE button to begin cooking.
5. With 6 minutes remaining, press START/PAUSE to pause the unit. Remove the basket from unit. Pour eggs over the sausage mixture and top with feta cheese. Reinsert basket in unit and press START/PAUSE to resume cooking.
6. When cooking is complete, remove basket from unit. Serve warm.

Banana Churros with Oatmeal

Serves: 2

|PREP TIME: 15 minutes
|COOK TIME: 15 minutes

For the Churros:
1 large yellow banana, peeled, cut in half lengthwise, then cut in half widthwise
2 tbsps. whole-wheat pastry flour
⅛ tsp. sea salt
2 tsps. oil (sunflower or melted coconut)
1 tsp. water
Cooking spray
1 tbsp. coconut sugar
½ tsp. cinnamon
For the Oatmeal:
¾ cup rolled oats
1½ cups water

To Make The Churros:
1. Put the 4 banana pieces in a medium-size bowl and add the flour and salt. Stir gently. Add the oil and water. Stir gently until evenly mixed. You may need to press some coating onto the banana pieces.
2. Install a crisper plate in a basket and spray with the oil spray. Put the banana pieces in the basket, then insert basket in unit.
3. Select Zone 1, select AIR FRY, set temperature to 350°F, and set time to 10 minutes. Press the START/PAUSE button to begin cooking.
4. With 5 minutes remaining, press START/PAUSE to pause the unit. Remove the basket from unit and flip the banana pieces over. Reinsert basket in unit and press START/PAUSE to resume cooking.
5. In a medium bowl, add the coconut sugar and cinnamon and stir to combine. When the banana pieces are nicely browned, spray with the oil and place in the cinnamon-sugar bowl. Toss gently with a spatula to coat the banana pieces with the mixture.
To Make The Oatmeal:
6. While the bananas are cooking, make the oatmeal. In a medium pot, bring the oats and water to a boil, then reduce to low heat. Simmer, stirring often, until all the water is absorbed, about 5 minutes. Put the oatmeal into two bowls.
7. Top the oatmeal with the coated banana pieces and serve immediately.

Parmesan Ranch Risotto

|PREP TIME: 10 minutes
|COOK TIME: 30 minutes

1 tbsp. olive oil
1 clove garlic, minced
1 tbsp. unsalted butter
1 onion, diced
¾ cup Arborio rice
2 cups chicken stock, boiling
½ cup Parmesan cheese, grated

1. Grease a 7 x 5-inch baking dish with olive oil and stir in the garlic, butter, and onion.
2. Install a crisper plate in a basket. Place baking dish in the basket, then insert basket in unit.
3. Select Zone 1, select BAKE, set temperature to 390°F, and set time to 30 minutes. Press the START/PAUSE button to begin cooking.
4. With 26 minutes remaining, press START/PAUSE to pause the unit. Remove the basket from unit and add the rice. Reinsert basket in unit and press START/PAUSE to resume cooking.
5. With 22 minutes remaining, press START/PAUSE to pause the unit. Remove the basket from unit and pour in the chicken stock. Reinsert basket in unit, turn the air fryer to 320ºF and press START/PAUSE to resume cooking.
6. When cooking is complete, scatter with cheese and serve.

Spinach with Scrambled Eggs

|PREP TIME: 10 minutes
|COOK TIME: 10 minutes

2 tbsps. olive oil
4 eggs, whisked
5 ounces (142 g) fresh spinach, chopped
1 medium tomato, chopped
1 tsp. fresh lemon juice
½ tsp. coarse salt
½ tsp. ground black pepper
½ cup of fresh basil, roughly chopped

1. Grease a 7 x 5-inch baking pan with the oil, tilting it to spread the oil around.
2. Add the remaining ingredients, apart from the basil leaves, whisking well until everything is completely combined.
3. Install a crisper plate in a basket. Place baking pan in the basket, then insert basket in unit.
4. Select Zone 1, select BAKE, set temperature to 350°F, and set time to 10 minutes. Press the START/PAUSE button to begin cooking.
5. When cooking is complete, top with fresh basil leaves before serving.

Mushroom and Squash Toast

Serves: 4

|PREP TIME: 10 minutes
|COOK TIME: 15 minutes

1 tbsp. olive oil
1 red bell pepper, cut into strips
2 green onions, sliced
1 cup sliced button or cremini mushrooms
1 small yellow squash, sliced
2 tbsps. softened butter
4 slices bread
½ cup soft goat cheese

1. Add the red pepper, green onions, mushrooms, and squash in a bowl, and stir well.
2. Spread the butter on the slices of bread.
3. Install a crisper plate in both baskets and brush with the olive oil. Place vegetables in the Zone 1 basket, then insert basket in unit. Place slices of bread in the Zone 2 basket, butter-side up, then insert basket in unit.
4. Select Zone 1, select AIR FRY, set temperature to 390°F, and set time to 15 minutes. Select Zone 2, select BAKE, set temperature to 350°F, and set time to 6 minutes. Select SMART FINISH. Press the START/PAUSE button to begin cooking.
5. When cooking is complete, transfer the bread slices to a plate. Top with goat cheese and vegetables. Serve warm.

Perfect Cheesy Eggs

Serves: 2

|PREP TIME: 10 minutes
|COOK TIME: 12 minutes

2 tsps. unsalted butter, softened
2-ounce ham, sliced thinly
4 large eggs, divided
3 tbsps. Parmesan cheese, grated finely
2 tsps. fresh chives, minced
2 tbsps. heavy cream
⅛ tsp. smoked paprika
Salt and black pepper, to taste

1. Grease a 5-inch pie pan with butter.
2. Whisk together 1 egg with cream, salt and black pepper in a bowl.
3. Place ham slices in the bottom of the pie pan and top with the egg mixture.
4. Crack the remaining eggs on top and season with smoked paprika, salt and black pepper. Top evenly with Parmesan cheese and chives.
5. Install a crisper plate in a basket. Place the pie pan in the basket, then insert basket in unit.
6. Select Zone 1, select BAKE, set temperature to 320°F, and set time to 12 minutes. Press the START/PAUSE button to begin cooking.
7. When cooking is complete, serve with toasted bread slices.

CHAPTER 2
Vegetables

Hasselback Potatoes

|PREP TIME: 20 minutes
|COOK TIME: 37 minutes

4 potatoes
2 tbsps. Parmesan cheese, shredded
1 tbsp. fresh chives, chopped
2 tbsps. olive oil

1. Cut slits along each potato about ¼-inch apart with a sharp knife, making sure slices should stay connected at the bottom.
2. Install a crisper plate in a basket. Coat the potatoes with olive oil and arrange in the basket, then insert basket in unit.
3. Select Zone 1, select AIR FRY, set temperature to 400°F, and set time to 37 minutes. Press the START/PAUSE button to begin cooking.
4. When cooking is complete, remove basket from unit. Transfer potatoes to a plate. Top with chives and Parmesan cheese to serve.

Buttered Broccoli

Serves: 4

|PREP TIME: 10 minutes
|COOK TIME: 10 minutes

4 cups fresh broccoli florets
2 tbsps. butter, melted
Salt and black pepper, to taste

1. Mix broccoli, butter, salt, and black pepper in a bowl and toss to coat well.
2. Install a crisper plate in a basket. Place broccoli florets in the basket, then insert basket in unit.
3. Select Zone 1, select AIR FRY, set temperature to 390°F, and set time to 10 minutes. Press the START/PAUSE button to begin cooking.
4. With 5 minutes remaining, press START/PAUSE to pause the unit. Remove the basket from unit and flip the broccoli florets over. Re-insert basket in unit and press START/PAUSE to resume cooking.
5. When cooking is complete, remove basket from unit. Transfer broccoli florets to a plate. Serve warm.

Breadcrumbs Stuffed Mushrooms

Serves: 4

|PREP TIME: 15 minutes
|COOK TIME: 15 minutes

1½ spelt bread slices
1 tbsp. flat-leaf parsley, finely chopped
16 small button mushrooms, stemmed and gills removed
1½ tbsps. olive oil
1 garlic clove, crushed
Salt and black pepper, to taste

1. Put the bread slices in a food processor and pulse until fine crumbs form.
2. Transfer the crumbs into a bowl and stir in the olive oil, garlic, parsley, salt, and black pepper.
3. Stuff the breadcrumbs mixture in each mushroom cap.
4. Install a crisper plate in both baskets. Place half of mushroom caps in a single layer in each basket.
5. Select Zone 1, select AIR FRY, set temperature to 390°F, and set time to 15 minutes. Select MATCH COOK to match Zone 2 settings to Zone 1. Select START/PAUSE to begin cooking.
6. When cooking is complete, transfer mushroom caps to a plate. Serve warm.

Almond Asparagus

Serves: 3

|PREP TIME: 15 minutes
|COOK TIME: 12 minutes

1 pound asparagus
⅓ cup almonds, sliced
2 tbsps. olive oil
2 tbsps. balsamic vinegar
Salt and black pepper, to taste

1. Mix asparagus, oil, vinegar, salt, and black pepper in a bowl and toss to coat well.
2. Install a crisper plate in a basket. Place asparagus and sprinkle the almond slices in the basket, then insert basket in unit.
3. Select Zone 1, select ROAST, set temperature to 390°F, and set time to 12 minutes. Press the START/PAUSE button to begin cooking.
4. With 6 minutes remaining, press START/PAUSE to pause the unit. Remove the basket from unit and flip the asparagus over. Reinsert basket in unit and press START/PAUSE to resume cooking.
5. When cooking is complete, remove basket from unit. Transfer asparagus to a plate. Serve warm.

Lemony Green Beans

|PREP TIME: 15 minutes
|COOK TIME: 10 minutes

1 pound green beans, trimmed and halved
1 tbsp. fresh lemon juice
1 tsp. unsalted butter, melted
¼ tsp. garlic powder

1. Mix all the ingredients in a bowl and toss to coat well.
2. Install a crisper plate in a basket. Place green beans in the basket, then insert basket in unit.
3. Select Zone 1, select AIR FRY, set temperature to 390°F, and set time to 10 minutes. Press the START/PAUSE button to begin cooking.
4. With 5 minutes remaining, press START/PAUSE to pause the unit. Remove the basket from unit and flip the green beans over. Reinsert basket in unit and press START/PAUSE to resume cooking.
5. When cooking is complete, remove basket from unit. Transfer green beans to a plate. Serve warm.

Caramelized Brussels Sprouts

|PREP TIME: 10 minutes
|COOK TIME: 20 minutes

1 pound Brussels sprouts, trimmed and halved
4 tsps. butter, melted
Salt and black pepper, to taste

1. Mix all the ingredients in a bowl and toss to coat well.
2. Install a crisper plate in a basket. Place Brussels sprouts in the basket, then insert basket in unit.
3. Select Zone 1, select AIR FRY, set temperature to 400°F, and set time to 20 minutes. Press the START/PAUSE button to begin cooking.
4. With 10 minutes remaining, press START/PAUSE to pause the unit. Remove the basket from unit and flip the Brussels sprouts over. Reinsert basket in unit and press START/PAUSE to resume cooking.
5. When cooking is complete, remove basket from unit. Transfer Brussels sprouts to a plate. Serve warm.

Versatile Stuffed Tomato

Serves: 4

|PREP TIME: 15 minutes
|COOK TIME: 24 minutes

4 tomatoes, tops and seeds removed
1 carrot, peeled and chopped
1 onion, chopped
1 cup frozen peas, thawed
2 cups cold cooked rice
1 tsp. olive oil
1 garlic clove, minced
1 tbsp. soy sauce

1. Heat olive oil in a skillet on low heat and add carrots, onions, peas and garlic.
2. Cook for about 2 minutes and stir in the soy sauce and rice.
3. Install a crisper plate in a basket. Stuff the rice mixture into the tomatoes and arrange in the basket, then insert basket in unit.
4. Select Zone 1, select BAKE, set temperature to 390°F, and set time to 22 minutes. Press the START/PAUSE button to begin cooking.
5. When cooking is complete, remove basket from unit. Transfer tomatoes to a plate. Serve warm.

Ritzy Vegetable Frittata

Serves: 2

|PREP TIME: 15 minutes
|COOK TIME: 24 minutes

4 eggs
¼ cup milk
Sea salt and ground black pepper, to taste
1 zucchini, sliced
½ bunch asparagus, sliced
½ cup mushrooms, sliced
½ cup spinach, shredded
½ cup red onion, sliced
½ tbsp. olive oil
5 tbsps. feta cheese, crumbled
4 tbsps. Cheddar cheese, grated
¼ bunch chives, minced

1. In a bowl, mix the eggs, milk, salt and pepper.
2. Over a medium heat, sauté the vegetables for 6 minutes with the olive oil in a nonstick pan.
3. Pour in the vegetables into two 5-inch cake pan followed by the egg mixture. Top with the feta and grated Cheddar.
4. Install a crisper plate in both baskets. Place one cake pan in each basket.
5. Select Zone 1, select BAKE, set temperature to 320°F, and set time to 18 minutes. Select MATCH COOK to match Zone 2 settings to Zone 1. Select START/PAUSE to begin cooking.
6. When cooking is complete, transfer cake pans to a plate and leave to cool for 5 minutes. Top with the minced chives and serve.

Turmeric Stuffed Okra

|PREP TIME: 15 minutes
|COOK TIME: 12 minutes

8 ounces large okras
¼ cup chickpea flour
¼ of onion, chopped
2 tbsps. coconut, grated freshly
1 tsp. garam masala powder
½ tsp. ground turmeric
½ tsp. red chili powder
½ tsp. ground cumin
Salt, to taste

1. Mix the flour, onion, grated coconut, and spices in a bowl and toss to coat well.
2. Install a crisper plate in a basket. Stuff the flour mixture into okras and arrange in the basket, then insert basket in unit.
3. Select Zone 1, select AIR FRY, set temperature to 390°F, and set time to 12 minutes. Press the START/PAUSE button to begin cooking.
4. With 6 minutes remaining, press START/PAUSE to pause the unit. Remove the basket from unit and flip the okras over. Reinsert basket in unit and press START/PAUSE to resume cooking.
5. When cooking is complete, remove basket from unit. Transfer okras to a plate. Serve warm.

Radish and Mozzarella Salad

|PREP TIME: 15 minutes
|COOK TIME: 30 minutes

1½ pounds radishes, trimmed and halved
½ pound fresh mozzarella, sliced
Salt and freshly ground black pepper, to taste
2 tbsps. olive oil
1 tsp. honey

1. Mix radishes, mozzarella, salt, black pepper and olive oil in a bowl and toss to coat well.
2. Install a crisper plate in a basket. Place radishes in the basket and spray with cooking spray, then insert basket in unit.
3. Select Zone 1, select AIR FRY, set temperature to 375°F, and set time to 30 minutes. Press the START/PAUSE button to begin cooking.
4. With 15 minutes remaining, press START/PAUSE to pause the unit. Remove the basket from unit and flip the radishes over. Reinsert basket in unit and press START/PAUSE to resume cooking.
5. When cooking is complete, remove basket from unit. Transfer radishes to a plate. Top with honey to serve.

Spiced Eggplant

|PREP TIME: 15 minutes
|COOK TIME: 15 minutes

2 medium eggplants, cubed
2 tbsps. butter, melted
2 tbsps. Parmesan cheese, shredded
1 tbsp. Maggi seasoning sauce
1 tsp. sumac
1 tsp. garlic powder
1 tsp. onion powder
Salt and ground black pepper, as required
1 tbsp. fresh lemon juice

1. Mix the eggplant cubes, butter, seasoning sauce and spices in a bowl and toss to coat well.
2. Install a crisper plate in a basket. Place eggplant cubes in the basket, then insert basket in unit.
3. Select Zone 1, select AIR FRY, set temperature to 390°F, and set time to 15 minutes. Press the START/PAUSE button to begin cooking.
4. With 8 minutes remaining, press START/PAUSE to pause the unit. Remove the basket from unit and shake for 10 seconds. Reinsert basket in unit and press START/PAUSE to resume cooking.
5. When cooking is complete, remove basket from unit. Transfer eggplant cubes to a plate and sprinkle with lemon juice and Parmesan cheese to serve.

Easy Glazed Carrots

|PREP TIME: 10 minutes
|COOK TIME: 16 minutes

3 cups carrots, peeled and cut into large chunks
1 tbsp. olive oil
1 tbsp. honey
Salt and black pepper, to taste

1. Mix all the ingredients in a bowl and toss to coat well.
2. Install a crisper plate in a basket. Place carrots in the basket, then insert basket in unit.
3. Select Zone 1, select AIR FRY, set temperature to 390°F, and set time to 16 minutes. Press the START/PAUSE button to begin cooking.
4. With 8 minutes remaining, press START/PAUSE to pause the unit. Remove the basket from unit and flip the carrots over. Reinsert basket in unit and press START/PAUSE to resume cooking.
5. When cooking is complete, remove basket from unit. Transfer carrots to a plate. Serve warm.

CHAPTER 3
Wraps, Tacos and Sandwich

Baked Cheese Sandwich

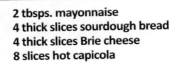

Serves: 2

PREP TIME: 5 minutes
COOK TIME: 8 minutes

2 tbsps. mayonnaise
4 thick slices sourdough bread
4 thick slices Brie cheese
8 slices hot capicola

1. Spread the mayonnaise on one side of each slice of bread.
2. Install a crisper plate in a basket. Place 2 slices of bread in the basket, mayonnaise-side down. Place the slices of Brie and capicola on the bread and cover with the remaining two slices of bread, mayonnaise-side up, then insert basket in unit.
3. Select Zone 1, select BAKE, set temperature to 350°F, and set time to 8 minutes. Press the START/PAUSE button to begin cooking, until the cheese has melted.
4. When cooking is complete, remove basket from unit. Serve immediately.

Turkey, Hummus and Cheese Wraps

Serves: 4

PREP TIME: 10 minutes
COOK TIME: 8 minutes

4 large whole wheat wraps
½ cup hummus
16 thin slices deli turkey
8 slices provolone cheese
1 cup fresh baby spinach, or more to taste

1. To assemble, place 2 tbsps. of hummus on each wrap and spread to within about a half inch from edges. Top with 4 slices of turkey and 2 slices of provolone. Finish with ¼ cup of baby spinach, or pile on as much as you like.
2. Roll up each wrap. You don't need to fold or seal the ends.
3. Install a crisper plate in both baskets. Place 2 wraps in each basket, seam-side down.
4. Select Zone 1, select AIR FRY, set temperature to 360°F, and set time to 8 minutes. Select MATCH COOK to match Zone 2 settings to Zone 1. Select START/PAUSE to begin cooking.
5. When cooking is complete, transfer wraps to a plate. Serve warm.

Cheesy Chicken Sandwich

|PREP TIME: 10 minutes
|COOK TIME: 6 minutes

⅓ cup chicken, cooked and shredded
2 Mozzarella slices
1 hamburger bun
¼ cup shredded cabbage
1 tsp. mayonnaise
2 tsps. butter, melted

1 tsp. olive oil
½ tsp. balsamic vinegar
¼ tsp. smoked paprika
¼ tsp. black pepper
¼ tsp. garlic powder
Pinch of salt

1. Brush some butter onto the outside of the hamburger bun.
2. In a bowl, coat the chicken with the garlic powder, salt, pepper, and paprika.
3. In a separate bowl, stir together the mayonnaise, olive oil, cabbage, and balsamic vinegar to make coleslaw.
4. Slice the bun in two. Start building the sandwich, starting with the chicken, followed by the Mozzarella, the coleslaw, and finally the top bun.
5. Install a crisper plate in a basket. Place sandwich in the basket, then insert basket in unit.
6. Select Zone 1, select BAKE, set temperature to 370°F, and set time to 6 minutes. Press the START/PAUSE button to begin cooking.
7. When cooking is complete, remove basket from unit. Serve immediately.

Bacon and Bell Pepper Sandwich

|PREP TIME: 10 minutes
|COOK TIME: 12 minutes

⅓ cup spicy barbecue sauce
2 tbsps. honey
8 slices cooked bacon, cut into thirds
1 red bell pepper, sliced

1 yellow bell pepper, sliced
3 pita pockets, cut in half
1¼ cups torn butter lettuce leaves
2 tomatoes, sliced

1. In a small bowl, combine the barbecue sauce and the honey. Brush this mixture lightly onto the bacon slices and the red and yellow pepper slices.
2. Install a crisper plate in both baskets. Place peppers in the Zone 1 basket, then insert basket in unit. Place bacon in the Zone 2 basket, then insert basket in unit.
3. Select Zone 1, select ROAST, set temperature to 390°F, and set time to 12 minutes. Select Zone 2, select AIR FRY, set temperature to 350°F, and set time to 6 minutes. Select SMART FINISH. Press the START/PAUSE button to begin cooking.
4. When the Zone 1 and 2 times reach 3 minutes, press START/PAUSE to pause the unit. Remove the baskets from unit and shake for 10 seconds. Reinsert baskets in unit and press START/PAUSE to resume cooking.
5. When cooking is complete, fill the pita halves with the bacon, peppers, any remaining barbecue sauce, lettuce, and tomatoes, and serve immediately.

Cajun-Style Fish Tacos

PREP TIME: 5 minutes
COOK TIME: 15 minutes

2 tsps. avocado oil
1 tbsp. Cajun seasoning
4 tilapia fillets
1 (14-ounce / 397-g) package coleslaw mix
12 corn tortillas
2 limes, cut into wedges

1. In a medium, shallow bowl, mix the avocado oil and the Cajun seasoning to make a marinade. Add the tilapia fillets and coat evenly.
2. Install a crisper plate in both baskets. Place 2 tilapia fillets in a single layer in each basket.
3. Select Zone 1, select AIR FRY, set temperature to 390°F, and set time to 15 minutes. Select MATCH COOK to match Zone 2 settings to Zone 1. Select START/PAUSE to begin cooking.
4. When the Zone 1 and 2 times reach 8 minutes, press START/PAUSE to pause the unit. Remove the baskets from unit and flip the tilapia fillets over. Reinsert baskets in unit and press START/PAUSE to resume cooking, until the fish is cooked and easily flakes with a fork.
5. When cooking is complete, transfer tilapia fillets to a plate. Assemble the tacos by placing some of the coleslaw mix in each tortilla. Add ⅓ of a tilapia fillet to each tortilla. Squeeze some lime juice over the top of each taco and serve.

Cheesy Greens Sandwich

PREP TIME: 15 minutes
COOK TIME: 8 minutes

1½ cups chopped mixed greens
2 garlic cloves, thinly sliced
2 tsps. olive oil
2 slices low-sodium low-fat Swiss cheese
4 slices low-sodium whole-wheat bread
Cooking spray

1. In a skillet over medium heat, add the greens, garlic, and olive oil. Cook for 4 to 5 minutes, until the vegetables are tender. Drain, if necessary.
2. Make 2 sandwiches, dividing half of the greens and 1 slice of Swiss cheese between 2 slices of bread. Lightly spray the outsides of the sandwiches with cooking spray.
3. Install a crisper plate in a basket. Place sandwiches in the basket, then insert basket in unit.
4. Select Zone 1, select BAKE, set temperature to 400°F, and set time to 8 minutes. Press the START/PAUSE button to begin cooking.
5. With 4 minutes remaining, press START/PAUSE to pause the unit. Remove the basket from unit and flip the sandwiches over. Reinsert basket in unit and press START/PAUSE to resume cooking, until the bread is toasted and the cheese melts.
6. When cooking is complete, remove basket from unit. Transfer sandwiches to a plate. Cut each sandwich in half and serve.

Nugget and Veggie Taco Wraps

Serves: 4

|PREP TIME: 5 minutes
|COOK TIME: 18 minutes

1 tbsp. water
4 pieces commercial vegan nuggets, chopped
1 small yellow onion, diced
1 small red bell pepper, chopped
2 cobs grilled corn kernels
4 large corn tortillas
Mixed greens, for garnish

1. Over a medium heat, sauté the nuggets in the water with the onion, corn kernels and bell pepper in a skillet, then remove from the heat.
2. Fill the tortillas with the nuggets and vegetables and fold them up.
3. Install a crisper plate in both baskets. Place 2 tortillas in a single layer in each basket.
4. Select Zone 1, select AIR FRY, set temperature to 400°F, and set time to 18 minutes. Select MATCH COOK to match Zone 2 settings to Zone 1. Select START/PAUSE to begin cooking.
5. When cooking is complete, transfer tortillas to a plate. Serve immediately, garnished with the mixed greens.

Banana Egg Oatmeal Sandwich

Serves: 4

|PREP TIME: 5 minutes
|COOK TIME: 8 minutes

½ cup cornflakes, crushed
¼ cup shredded coconut
8 slices oat nut bread or any whole-grain, oversize bread
6 tbsps. peanut butter
2 medium bananas, cut into ½-inch-thick slices
6 tbsps. pineapple preserves
1 egg, beaten
Cooking spray

1. In a shallow dish, mix the cornflake crumbs and coconut.
2. For each sandwich, spread one bread slice with 1½ tbsps. of peanut butter. Top with banana slices. Spread another bread slice with 1½ tbsps. of preserves. Combine to make a sandwich.
3. Using a pastry brush, brush top of sandwich lightly with beaten egg. Sprinkle with about 1½ tbsps. of crumb coating, pressing it in to make it stick. Spray with cooking spray.
4. Turn sandwich over and repeat to coat and spray the other side.
5. Install a crisper plate in both baskets. Place 2 sandwiches in a single layer in each basket.
6. Select Zone 1, select BAKE, set temperature to 360°F, and set time to 8 minutes. Select MATCH COOK to match Zone 2 settings to Zone 1. Select START/PAUSE to begin cooking, until coating is golden brown and crispy.
7. When cooking is complete, transfer sandwiches to a plate. Cut the cooked sandwiches in half and serve warm.

Tuna and Lettuce Wraps

PREP TIME: 10 minutes
COOK TIME: 7 minutes

cooking spray
1 pound (454 g) fresh tuna steak, cut into 1-inch cubes
1 tbsp. grated fresh ginger
2 garlic cloves, minced
½ tsp. toasted sesame oil
4 low-sodium whole-wheat tortillas
¼ cup low-fat mayonnaise
2 cups shredded romaine lettuce
1 red bell pepper, thinly sliced

1. Preheat the air fryer to 390ºF (199ºC).
2. In a medium bowl, mix the tuna, ginger, garlic, and sesame oil. Let it stand for 10 minutes.
3. Install a crisper plate in a basket and spray with cooking spray. Place tuna in the basket, then insert basket in unit.
4. Select Zone 1, select AIR FRY, set temperature to 390°F, and set time to 7 minutes. Press the START/PAUSE button to begin cooking.
5. With 3 minutes remaining, press START/PAUSE to pause the unit. Remove the basket from unit and shake for 10 seconds. Reinsert basket in unit and press START/PAUSE to resume cooking.
6. When cooking is complete, remove basket from unit.
7. Make the wraps with the tuna, tortillas, mayonnaise, lettuce, and bell pepper. Serve immediately.

Lettuce Fajita Meatball Wraps

PREP TIME: 10 minutes
COOK TIME: 14 minutes

1 pound (454 g) 85% lean ground beef
½ cup salsa, plus more for serving
¼ cup chopped onions
¼ cup diced green or red bell peppers
1 large egg, beaten
1 tsp. fine sea salt
½ tsp. chili powder
½ tsp. ground cumin
1 clove garlic, minced
Cooking spray
For Serving:
8 leaves Boston lettuce
Pico de gallo or salsa
Lime slices

1. In a large bowl, mix together all the ingredients until well combined.
2. Shape the meat mixture into eight 1-inch balls.
3. Install a crisper plate in both baskets and spray with cooking spray. Place half of the balls in a single layer in each basket.
4. Select Zone 1, select AIR FRY, set temperature to 350°F, and set time to 14 minutes. Select MATCH COOK to match Zone 2 settings to Zone 1. Select START/PAUSE to begin cooking.
5. When the Zone 1 and 2 times reach 8 minutes, press START/PAUSE to pause the unit. Remove the baskets from unit and flip the balls over. Reinsert baskets in unit and press START/PAUSE to resume cooking.
6. When cooking is complete, serve each meatball on a lettuce leaf, topped with pico de gallo or salsa. Serve with lime slices.

Smoky Chicken Sandwich

Serves: 2

|PREP TIME: 10 minutes
|COOK TIME: 11 minutes

2 boneless, skinless chicken breasts (8 ounces / 227 g each), sliced horizontally in half and separated into 4 thinner cutlets
Kosher salt and freshly ground black pepper, to taste
½ cup all-purpose flour
3 large eggs, lightly beaten
½ cup dried bread crumbs
1 tbsp. smoked paprika
Cooking spray
½ cup marinara sauce
6 ounces (170 g) smoked Mozzarella cheese, grated
2 store-bought soft, sesame-seed hamburger or Italian buns, split

1. Season the chicken cutlets all over with salt and pepper. Set up three shallow bowls: Place the flour in the first bowl, the eggs in the second, and stir together the bread crumbs and smoked paprika in the third. Coat the chicken pieces in the flour, then dip fully in the egg. Dredge in the paprika bread crumbs, then transfer to a wire rack set over a baking sheet and spray both sides liberally with cooking spray.
2. Install a crisper plate in both baskets. Place 2 chicken cutlets in each basket.
3. Select Zone 1, select AIR FRY, set temperature to 350°F, and set time to 20 minutes. Select MATCH COOK to match Zone 2 settings to Zone 1. Select START/PAUSE to begin cooking.
4. When the Zone 1 and 2 times reach 6 minutes, press START/PAUSE to pause the unit. Remove the baskets from unit. Spread each cutlet with 2 tbsps. of the marinara sauce and sprinkle with one-quarter of the smoked Mozzarella. Reinsert baskets in unit and press START/PAUSE to resume cooking.
5. When cooking is complete, transfer cutlets to a plate, stack on top of each other, and place 2 cutlets inside a bun. Serve the sandwiches warm.

Vegetable and Fish Tacos

Serves: 4

|PREP TIME: 10 minutes
|COOK TIME: 9 minutes

1 pound (454 g) white fish fillets
2 tsps. olive oil
3 tbsps. freshly squeezed lemon juice, divided
1½ cups chopped red cabbage
1 large carrot, grated
½ cup low-sodium salsa
⅓ cup low-fat Greek yogurt
4 soft low-sodium whole-wheat tortillas

1. Brush the fish with the olive oil and sprinkle with 1 tbsp. of lemon juice.
2. Install a crisper plate in a basket. Place fish in the basket, then insert basket in unit.
3. Select Zone 1, select AIR FRY, set temperature to 400°F, and set time to 9 minutes. Press the START/PAUSE button to begin cooking, until the fish just flakes when tested with a fork.
4. Meanwhile, in a medium bowl, stir together the remaining 2 tbsps. of lemon juice, the red cabbage, carrot, salsa, and yogurt.
5. When cooking is complete, remove basket from unit. Transfer the fish to a plate and break it up into large pieces.
6. Offer the fish, tortillas, and the cabbage mixture, and let each person assemble a taco.
7. Serve warm.

CHAPTER 4
Poultry

Bacon Wrapped Chicken Breasts

Serves: 4

|PREP TIME: 20 minutes
|COOK TIME: 28 minutes

6-7 Fresh basil leaves
2 tbsps. water
2 (8-ounces) chicken breasts, cut each breast in half horizontally
12 bacon strips
2 tbsps. fish sauce
1 tbsp. palm sugar
Salt and ground black pepper, as required
1½ tsps. honey

1. Cook the palm sugar in a small heavy-bottomed pan over medium-low heat for about 3 minutes until caramelized.
2. Stir in the basil, fish sauce and water and dish out in a bowl.
3. Season each chicken breast with salt and black pepper and coat with the palm sugar mixture.
4. Refrigerate to marinate for about 6 hours and wrap each chicken piece with 3 bacon strips. Dip into the honey.
5. Install a crisper plate in a basket. Place chicken breasts in the basket, then insert basket in unit.
6. Select Zone 1, select ROAST, set temperature to 390°F, and set time to 25 minutes. Press the START/PAUSE button to begin cooking.
7. With 10 minutes remaining, press START/PAUSE to pause the unit. Remove the basket from unit and flip the chicken breasts over. Reinsert basket in unit and press START/PAUSE to resume cooking.
8. When cooking is complete, remove basket from unit. Transfer chicken breasts to a plate. Serve warm.

Juicy Herbed Drumsticks

Serves: 4

|PREP TIME: 10 minutes
|COOK TIME: 22 minutes

½ tbsp. fresh rosemary, minced
1 tbsp. fresh thyme, minced
4 boneless chicken drumsticks
¼ cup Dijon mustard
1 tbsp. honey
2 tbsps. olive oil
Salt and freshly ground black pepper, to taste

1. Mix all the ingredients in a bowl except the drumsticks until well combined.
2. Stir in the drumsticks and coat generously with the mixture.
3. Cover and refrigerate to marinate overnight.
4. Install a crisper plate in a basket. Place drumsticks in the basket, then insert basket in unit.
5. Select Zone 1, select AIR FRY, set temperature to 390°F, and set time to 22 minutes. Press the START/PAUSE button to begin cooking.
6. With 10 minutes remaining, press START/PAUSE to pause the unit. Remove the basket from unit and flip the drumsticks over. Reinsert basket in unit and press START/PAUSE to resume cooking.
7. When cooking is complete, remove basket from unit. Transfer drumsticks to a plate. Serve warm.

Sweet and Spicy Chicken Drumsticks

|PREP TIME: 15 minutes
|COOK TIME: 20 minutes

4 (6-ounces) chicken drumsticks
1 garlic clove, crushed
1 tbsp. mustard
2 tsps. brown sugar
1 tsp. cayenne pepper
1 tsp. red chili powder
Salt and ground black pepper, as required
1 tbsp. vegetable oil

1. Mix garlic, mustard, brown sugar, oil, and spices in a bowl.
2. Rub the chicken drumsticks with marinade and refrigerate for about 30 minutes.
3. Install a crisper plate in a basket. Place drumsticks in the basket, then insert basket in unit.
4. Select Zone 1, select AIR FRY, set temperature to 390°F, and set time to 20 minutes. Press the START/PAUSE button to begin cooking.
5. With 10 minutes remaining, press START/PAUSE to pause the unit. Remove the basket from unit and flip the drumsticks over. Reinsert basket in unit and press START/PAUSE to resume cooking.
6. When cooking is complete, remove basket from unit. Transfer drumsticks to a plate. Serve warm.

Buffalo Chicken Wings

|PREP TIME: 20 minutes
|COOK TIME: 22 minutes

2 pounds chicken wings, cut into drumettes and flats
1 tsp. chicken seasoning
1 tsp. garlic powder
Ground black pepper, to taste
1 tbsp. olive oil
¼ cup red hot sauce
2 tbsps. low-sodium soy sauce

1. Season each chicken wing evenly with chicken seasoning, garlic powder, and black pepper.
2. Install a crisper plate in a basket. Place chicken wings in the basket and drizzle with olive oil, then insert basket in unit.
3. Select Zone 1, select ROAST, set temperature to 390°F, and set time to 22 minutes. Press the START/PAUSE button to begin cooking.
4. With 10 minutes remaining, press START/PAUSE to pause the unit. Remove the basket from unit. Pour the red hot sauce and soy sauce on the chicken wings and toss to coat well. Reinsert basket in unit and press START/PAUSE to resume cooking.
5. When cooking is complete, remove basket from unit. Transfer chicken wings to a plate. Serve warm.

Surprisingly Tasty Chicken

Serves: 4

|PREP TIME: 10 minutes
|COOK TIME: 40 minutes

½ whole chicken (about 1½ pounds)
1 pound small potatoes
Salt and black pepper, to taste
1 tbsp. olive oil, scrubbed

1. Season the chicken with salt and black pepper.
2. Mix potato, oil, salt and black pepper in a bowl and toss to coat well
3. Install a crisper plate in both baskets. Place chicken in the Zone 1 basket, then insert basket in unit. Place potatoes in the Zone 2 basket, then insert basket in unit.
4. Select Zone 1, select ROAST, set temperature to 390°F, and set time to 40 minutes. Select Zone 2, select AIR FRY, set temperature to 390°F, and set time to 30 minutes. Select SMART FINISH. Press the START/PAUSE button to begin cooking.
5. When the Zone 1 and 2 times reach 15 minutes, press START/PAUSE to pause the unit. Remove the baskets from unit and flip the chicken and potatoes. Reinsert baskets in unit and press START/PAUSE to resume cooking.
6. When cooking is complete, serve chicken with potatoes.

Breaded Chicken Tenderloins

Serves: 4

|PREP TIME: 15 minutes
|COOK TIME: 26 minutes

1 egg, beaten
½ cup breadcrumbs
8 skinless, boneless chicken tenderloins
2 tbsps. vegetable oil

1. Whisk the egg in a bowl and mix vegetable oil and breadcrumbs in another bowl.
2. Dip the chicken tenderloins into the whisked egg and then coat with the breadcrumb mixture.
3. Install a crisper plate in both baskets. Place 4 chicken tenderloins in a single layer in each basket.
4. Select Zone 1, select AIR FRY, set temperature to 360°F, and set time to 26 minutes. Select MATCH COOK to match Zone 2 settings to Zone 1. Select START/PAUSE to begin cooking.
5. When the Zone 1 and 2 times reach 12 minutes, press START/PAUSE to pause the unit. Remove the baskets from unit and flip the chicken tenderloins over. Reinsert baskets in unit and press START/PAUSE to resume cooking.
6. When cooking is complete, transfer chicken tenderloins to a plate. Serve warm.

Cajun Chicken Thighs

Serves: 4

|PREP TIME: 15 minutes
|COOK TIME: 25 minutes

½ cup all-purpose flour
1 egg
4 (4-ounces) skin-on chicken thighs
1½ tbsps. Cajun seasoning
1 tsp. seasoning salt
1 pound green beans, trimmed and halved
1 tsp. unsalted butter, melted
¼ tsp. garlic powder

1. Mix the flour, Cajun seasoning and salt in a bowl.
2. Whisk the egg in another bowl and coat the chicken thighs with the flour mixture.
3. Dip into the egg and dredge again into the flour mixture.
4. Mix the green beans, butter and garlic powder in a medium bowl and toss to coat well.
5. Install a crisper plate in both baskets. Place chicken thighs in the Zone 1 basket, skin side down, then insert basket in unit. Place green beans in the Zone 2 basket, then insert basket in unit.
6. Select Zone 1, select AIR FRY, set temperature to 390°F, and set time to 25 minutes. Select Zone 2, select AIR FRY, set temperature to 390°F, and set time to 15 minutes. Select SMART FINISH. Press the START/PAUSE button to begin cooking.
7. When the Zone 1 and 2 times reach 8 minutes, press START/PAUSE to pause the unit. Remove the baskets from unit and shake for 10 seconds. Reinsert baskets in unit and press START/PAUSE to resume cooking.
8. When cooking is complete, serve chicken thighs with green beans.

Glazed Chicken Wings

Serves: 4

|PREP TIME: 10 minutes
|COOK TIME: 18 minutes

8 chicken wings
2 tbsps. all-purpose flour
1 tsp. garlic, chopped finely
1 tbsp. fresh lemon juice
1 tbsp. soy sauce
½ tsp. dried oregano, crushed
Salt and freshly ground black pepper, to taste

1. Mix all the ingredients except wings in a large bowl.
2. Coat wings generously with the marinade and refrigerate for about 2 hours.
3. Remove the chicken wings from marinade and sprinkle with flour evenly.
4. Install a crisper plate in a basket. Place wings in the basket, then insert basket in unit.
5. Select Zone 1, select AIR FRY, set temperature to 390°F, and set time to 18 minutes. Press the START/PAUSE button to begin cooking.
6. With 8 minutes remaining, press START/PAUSE to pause the unit. Remove the basket from unit and flip the wings over. Reinsert basket in unit and press START/PAUSE to resume cooking.
7. When cooking is complete, remove basket from unit. Transfer wings to a plate. Serve hot.

Tandoori Chicken Legs

Serves: 4

|PREP TIME: 15 minutes
|COOK TIME: 22 minutes

4 chicken legs
4 tbsps. hung curd
3 tbsps. fresh lemon juice
3 tsps. ginger paste
3 tsps. garlic paste
Salt, as required
2 tbsps. tandoori masala powder

2 tsps. red chili powder
1 tsp. garam masala powder
1 tsp. ground cumin
1 tsp. ground coriander
1 tsp. ground turmeric
Ground black pepper, as required
Pinch of orange food color

1. Mix chicken legs, lemon juice, ginger paste, garlic paste, and salt in a bowl.
2. Combine the curd, spices, and food color in another bowl.
3. Add the chicken legs into bowl and coat generously with the spice mixture.
4. Cover the bowl of chicken and refrigerate for at least 12 hours.
5. Install a crisper plate in a basket. Place chicken legs in the basket, then insert basket in unit.
6. Select Zone 1, select ROAST, set temperature to 390°F, and set time to 22 minutes. Press the START/PAUSE button to begin cooking.
7. With 10 minutes remaining, press START/PAUSE to pause the unit. Remove the basket from unit and flip the chicken legs over. Reinsert basket in unit and press START/PAUSE to resume cooking.
8. When cooking is complete, remove basket from unit. Transfer chicken legs to a plate. Serve warm.

(Note: Hung curd - Hung curd is nothing but yogurt drained of all its water. It can be made very easily at home.)

Sausage Stuffed Chicken

Serves: 4

|PREP TIME: 10 minutes
|COOK TIME: 22 minutes

4 (4-ounce) skinless, boneless chicken breasts
4 sausages, casing removed
2 tbsps. mustard sauce

1. Roll each chicken breast with a rolling pin for about 1 minute.
2. Arrange 1 sausage over each chicken breast and roll up. Secure with toothpicks.
3. Install a crisper plate in a basket. Place stuffed chicken breasts in the basket, then insert basket in unit.
4. Select Zone 1, select AIR FRY, set temperature to 390°F, and set time to 22 minutes. Press the START/PAUSE button to begin cooking.
5. With 10 minutes remaining, press START/PAUSE to pause the unit. Remove the basket from unit and flip the chicken breasts over. Reinsert basket in unit and press START/PAUSE to resume cooking.
6. When cooking is complete, remove basket from unit. Transfer chicken breasts to a plate and serve with mustard sauce.

Cheesy Chicken Breasts with Zucchini

|PREP TIME: 20 minutes
|COOK TIME: 25 minutes

2 (6-ounces) chicken breasts
1 egg, beaten
4 ounces breadcrumbs
1 tbsp. fresh basil
¼ cup grated Parmesan cheese, divided
2 tbsps. vegetable oil
¼ cup pasta sauce

1 small zucchini, sliced into ½-inch thick rounds
1 tbsp. olive oil, divided
2 tbsps. fat-free Italian dressing
Salt, to taste

1. Whisk egg in a bowl and mix breadcrumbs, vegetable oil and basil in another bowl.
2. Dip the chicken breasts into the egg and then coat with the breadcrumb mixture.
3. Mix zucchini, 2 tbsps. Parmesan cheese, olive oil, Italian dressing, and salt in a medium bowl and toss to coat well.
4. Install a crisper plate in both baskets. Place chicken breasts in the Zone 1 basket, then insert basket in unit. Place zucchini slices in the Zone 2 basket, then insert basket in unit.
5. Select Zone 1, select AIR FRY, set temperature to 390°F, and set time to 25 minutes. Select Zone 2, select AIR FRY, set temperature to 390°F, and set time to 20 minutes. Select SMART FINISH. Press the START/PAUSE button to begin cooking.
6. When the Zone 1 and Zone 2 times reach 10 minutes, press START/PAUSE and remove baskets from unit. In Zone 1, top the chicken breasts with pasta sauce and the remaining Parmesan cheese. In Zone 2, shake for 10 seconds. Reinsert baskets in unit and press START/PAUSE to resume cooking.
7. When cooking is complete, serve chicken breasts with zucchini.

Cheese Stuffed Turkey Breasts

|PREP TIME: 15 minutes
|COOK TIME: 20 minutes

2 (8-ounces) turkey breast fillets, skinless and boneless, each cut into 2 pieces
4 cheddar cheese slices
1 tbsp. fresh parsley, minced
4 bacon slices
Salt and black pepper, to taste

1. Make a slit in each turkey piece horizontally and season with salt and black pepper.
2. Insert cheddar cheese slice into the slits and sprinkle with parsley.
3. Wrap each turkey piece with one bacon slice.
4. Install a crisper plate in a basket. Place turkey pieces in the basket, then insert basket in unit.
5. Select Zone 1, select AIR FRY, set temperature to 390°F, and set time to 20 minutes. Press the START/PAUSE button to begin cooking.
6. With 10 minutes remaining, press START/PAUSE to pause the unit. Remove the basket from unit and flip the turkey pieces over. Reinsert basket in unit and press START/PAUSE to resume cooking.
7. When cooking is complete, remove basket from unit. Transfer turkey pieces to a plate. Serve warm.

CHAPTER 5
Lamb

Roasted Lamb Leg

|PREP TIME: 15 minutes
|COOK TIME: 1 hour

2½ pounds half lamb leg roast, slits carved
2 garlic cloves, sliced into smaller slithers
1 tbsp. dried rosemary
1 tbsp. olive oil
Cracked Himalayan rock salt and cracked peppercorns, to taste

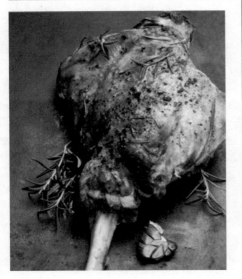

1. Insert the garlic slithers in the slits and brush with rosemary, oil, salt, and black pepper.
2. Install a crisper plate in a basket. Place the lamb in the basket, then insert basket in unit.
3. Select Zone 1, select ROAST, set temperature to 390°F, and set time to 1 hour. Press the START/PAUSE button to begin cooking.
4. With 30 minutes remaining, press START/PAUSE to pause the unit. Remove the basket from unit and flip the lamb over. Reinsert basket in unit and press START/PAUSE to resume cooking.
5. When cooking is complete, remove basket from unit. Transfer the to a plate. Serve warm.

Garlicky Lamb Chops

|PREP TIME: 20 minutes
|COOK TIME: 17 minutes

1 tbsp. fresh oregano, chopped
1 tbsp. fresh thyme, chopped
8 (4-ounce) lamb chops
¼ cup olive oil, divided
1 bulb garlic, halved
Salt and black pepper, to taste

1. Rub the garlic bulb halves with about 2 tbsps. of the olive oil.
2. Mix remaining oil, herbs, salt and black pepper in a large bowl. Coat the lamb chops with about 1 tbsp. of the herb mixture.
3. Install a crisper plate in both baskets. Place 4 lamb chops and garlic bulb halve in a single layer in each basket.
4. Select Zone 1, select ROAST, set temperature to 390°F, and set time to 17 minutes. Select MATCH COOK to match Zone 2 settings to Zone 1. Select START/PAUSE to begin cooking.
5. When the Zone 1 and 2 times reach 8 minutes, press START/PAUSE to pause the unit. Remove the baskets from unit and flip the lamb chops over. Reinsert baskets in unit and press START/PAUSE to resume cooking.
6. When cooking is complete, transfer lamb chops to a plate and serve with herb mixture.

Herbed Lamb Chops

Serves: 2

|PREP TIME: 10 minutes
|COOK TIME: 15 minutes

4 (4-ounces) lamb chops
1 tbsp. fresh lemon juice
1 tbsp. olive oil
1 tsp. dried rosemary
1 tsp. dried thyme
1 tsp. dried oregano
½ tsp. ground cumin
½ tsp. ground coriander
Salt and black pepper, to taste

1. Mix the lemon juice, oil, herbs, and spices in a large bowl.
2. Coat the chops generously with the herb mixture and refrigerate to marinate for about 1 hour.
3. Install a crisper plate in a basket. Place chops in the basket, then insert basket in unit.
4. Select Zone 1, select AIR FRY, set temperature to 390°F, and set time to 15 minutes. Press the START/PAUSE button to begin cooking.
5. With 7 minutes remaining, press START/PAUSE to pause the unit. Remove the basket from unit and flip the chops over. Reinsert basket in unit and press START/PAUSE to resume cooking.
6. When cooking is complete, remove basket from unit. Transfer chops to a plate. Serve warm.

Lamb Leg with Brussels Sprouts

Serves: 6

|PREP TIME: 20 minutes
|COOK TIME: 1 hour

2¼ pounds leg of lamb
1 tbsp. fresh rosemary, minced
1 tbsp. fresh lemon thyme
1½ pounds Brussels sprouts, trimmed
3 tbsps. olive oil, divided
1 garlic clove, minced
Salt and ground black pepper, as required
2 tbsps. honey

1. Make slits in the leg of lamb with a sharp knife.
2. Mix 2 tbsps. of oil, herbs, garlic, salt, and black pepper in a bowl.
3. Coat the leg of lamb with oil mixture generously.
4. Install a crisper plate in both baskets. Place leg of lamb in the Zone 1 basket, then insert basket in unit. Coat the Brussels sprouts evenly with the remaining oil and honey and arrange in the Zone 2 basket, then insert basket in unit.
5. Select Zone 1, select ROAST, set temperature to 400°F, and set time to 1 hour. Select Zone 2, select AIR FRY, set temperature to 400°F, and set time to 28 minutes. Select SMART FINISH. Press the START/PAUSE button to begin cooking.
6. When cooking is complete, serve lamb with vegetables.

Za'atar Lamb Loin Chops

Serves: 4

|PREP TIME: 10 minutes
|COOK TIME: 16 minutes

8 (3½-ounces) bone-in lamb loin chops, trimmed
3 garlic cloves, crushed
1 tbsp. fresh lemon juice
1 tsp. olive oil
1 tbsp. Za'ataro
Salt and black pepper, to taste

1. Mix the garlic, lemon juice, oil, Za'atar, salt, and black pepper in a large bowl.
2. Coat the chops generously with the herb mixture.
3. Install a crisper plate in both baskets. Place 4 chops in a single layer in each basket.
4. Select Zone 1, select ROAST, set temperature to 400°F, and set time to 16 minutes. Select MATCH COOK to match Zone 2 settings to Zone 1. Select START/PAUSE to begin cooking.
5. When the Zone 1 and 2 times reach 8 minutes, press START/PAUSE to pause the unit. Remove the baskets from unit and flip the chops over. Reinsert baskets in unit and press START/PAUSE to resume cooking.
6. When cooking is complete, transfer chops to a plate. Serve warm.

(Note: Za'atar - Za'atar is generally made with ground dried thyme, oregano, marjoram, or some combination thereof, mixed with toasted sesame seeds, and salt, though other spices such as sumac might also be added. Some commercial varieties also include roasted flour.)

Nut Crusted Rack of Lamb

Serves: 6

|PREP TIME: 15 minutes
|COOK TIME: 35 minutes

1¾ pounds rack of lamb
1 egg
1 tbsp. breadcrumbs
3-ounce almonds, chopped finely
1 tbsp. fresh rosemary, chopped
1 tbsp. olive oil
1 garlic clove, minced
Salt and black pepper, to taste

1. Mix garlic, olive oil, salt and black pepper in a bowl.
2. Whisk the egg in a shallow dish and mix breadcrumbs, almonds and rosemary in another shallow dish.
3. Coat the rack of lamb with garlic mixture evenly, dip into the egg and dredge into the breadcrumb mixture.
4. Install a crisper plate in a basket. Place rack of lamb in the basket, then insert basket in unit.
5. Select Zone 1, select ROAST, set temperature to 390°F, and set time to 35minutes. Press the START/PAUSE button to begin cooking.
6. With 15 minutes remaining, press START/PAUSE to pause the unit. Remove the basket from unit and flip the rack of lamb over. Reinsert basket in unit and press START/PAUSE to resume cooking.
7. When cooking is complete, remove basket from unit. Transfer the rack of lamb to a plate. Serve warm.

Greek Lamb Pita Pockets

|PREP TIME: 15 minutes
|COOK TIME: 10 minutes

For the Dressing:
1 cup plain yogurt
1 tbsp. lemon juice
1 tsp. dried dill weed, crushed
1 tsp. ground oregano
½ tsp. salt
For the Meatballs:
½ pound (227 g) ground lamb
1 tbsp. diced onion
1 tsp. dried parsley
1 tsp. dried dill weed, crushed
¼ tsp. oregano

¼ tsp. coriander
¼ tsp. ground cumin
¼ tsp. salt
4 pita halves
Suggested Toppings:
1 red onion, slivered
1 medium cucumber, deseeded, thinly sliced
Crumbled Feta cheese
Sliced black olives
Chopped fresh peppers

1. Stir the dressing ingredients together in a small bowl and refrigerate while preparing lamb.
2. Combine all meatball ingredients in a large bowl and stir to distribute seasonings.
3. Shape meat mixture into 12 small meatballs, rounded or slightly flattened if you prefer.
4. Install a crisper plate in both baskets. Place half of the meatballs in a single layer in each basket.
5. Select Zone 1, select AIR FRY, set temperature to 390°F, and set time to 10 minutes. Select MATCH COOK to match Zone 2 settings to Zone 1. Select START/PAUSE to begin cooking.
6. When the Zone 1 and 2 times reach 5 minutes, press START/PAUSE to pause the unit. Remove the baskets from unit and flip the meatballs over. Reinsert baskets in unit and press START/PAUSE to resume cooking.
7. When cooking is complete, transfer meatballs and drain on paper towels.
8. To serve, pile meatballs and the choice of toppings in pita pockets and drizzle with dressing.

Spiced Lamb Steaks

|PREP TIME: 15 minutes
|COOK TIME: 15 minutes

½ onion, roughly chopped
1½ pounds boneless lamb sirloin steaks
5 garlic cloves, peeled
1 tbsp. fresh ginger, peeled
1 tsp. garam masala
1 tsp. ground fennel
½ tsp. ground cumin
½ tsp. ground cinnamon
½ tsp. cayenne pepper
Salt and black pepper, to taste

1. Put the onion, garlic, ginger, and spices in a blender and pulse until smooth.
2. Coat the lamb steaks with this mixture on both sides and refrigerate to marinate for about 24 hours.
3. Install a crisper plate in a basket. Place lamb steaks in the basket, then insert basket in unit.
4. Select Zone 1, select ROAST, set temperature to 390°F, and set time to 15 minutes. Press the START/PAUSE button to begin cooking.
5. With 8 minutes remaining, press START/PAUSE to pause the unit. Remove the basket from unit and flip the lamb steaks over. Reinsert basket in unit and press START/PAUSE to resume cooking.
6. When cooking is complete, remove basket from unit. Transfer lamb steaks to a plate. Serve warm.

Roasted Lamb with Potatoes

PREP TIME: 20 minutes
COOK TIME: 30 minutes

½ pound lamb meat
2 small potatoes, peeled and halved
½ small onion, peeled and halved
1 garlic clove, crushed
½ tbsp. dried rosemary, crushed
1 tsp. olive oil

1. Rub the lamb evenly with garlic and rosemary.
2. Add potatoes in a large bowl and stir in the olive oil and onions.
3. Install a crisper plate in both baskets. Place lamb in the Zone 1 basket, then insert basket in unit. Place vegetables in the Zone 2 basket, then insert basket in unit.
4. Select Zone 1, select ROAST, set temperature to 390°F, and set time to 25 minutes. Select Zone 2, select ROAST, set temperature to 400°F, and set time to 30 minutes. Select SMART FINISH. Press the START/PAUSE button to begin cooking.
5. When the Zone 1 and 2 times reach 15 minutes, press START/PAUSE to pause the unit. Remove the baskets from unit and flip the lamb and vegetables over. Reinsert baskets in unit and press START/PAUSE to resume cooking.
6. When cooking is complete, serve lamb with vegetables.

Lamb Meatballs with Tomato Sauce

PREP TIME: 20 minutes
COOK TIME: 27 minutes

For the Meatballs:
½ small onion, finely diced
1 clove garlic, minced
1 pound (454 g) ground lamb
2 tbsps. fresh parsley, finely chopped (plus more for garnish)
2 tsps. fresh oregano, finely chopped
2 tbsps. milk
1 egg yolk
Salt and freshly ground black pepper, to taste
½ cup crumbled feta cheese, for garnish

For the Tomato Sauce:
2 tbsps. butter
1 clove garlic, smashed
Pinch crushed red pepper flakes
¼ tsp. ground cinnamon
1 (28-ounce / 794-g) can crushed tomatoes
Salt, to taste
Cooking spray

1. Combine all ingredients for the meatballs in a large bowl and mix just until everything is combined. Shape the mixture into 1½-inch balls or shape the meat between two spoons to make quenelles.
2. Start the quick tomato sauce. Put the butter, garlic and red pepper flakes in a sauté pan and heat over medium heat on the stovetop. Let the garlic sizzle a little, but before the butter browns, add the cinnamon and tomatoes. Bring to a simmer and simmer for 15 minutes. Season with salt.
3. Install a crisper plate in both baskets. Place half of the meatballs in a single layer in each basket. Spray with cooking spray.
4. Select Zone 1, select AIR FRY, set temperature to 400°F, and set time to 12 minutes. Select MATCH COOK to match Zone 2 settings to Zone 1. Select START/PAUSE to begin cooking.
5. When the Zone 1 and 2 times reach 6 minutes, press START/PAUSE to pause the unit. Remove the baskets from unit and flip the meatballs over. Reinsert baskets in unit and press START/PAUSE to resume cooking.
6. When cooking is complete, transfer meatballs to a plate. To serve, spoon a pool of the tomato sauce onto plates and add the meatballs. Sprinkle the feta cheese on top and garnish with more fresh parsley. Serve immediately.

Greek Lamb Rack

|PREP TIME: 5 minutes
|COOK TIME: 14 minutes

¼ cup freshly squeezed lemon juice
1 tsp. oregano
2 tsps. minced fresh rosemary
1 tsp. minced fresh thyme
2 tbsps. minced garlic
Salt and freshly ground black pepper, to taste
2 to 4 tbsps. olive oil
1 lamb rib rack (7 to 8 ribs)

1. In a small mixing bowl, combine the lemon juice, oregano, rosemary, thyme, garlic, salt, pepper, and olive oil and mix well.
2. Rub the mixture over the lamb, covering all the meat.
3. Install a crisper plate in a basket. Place rack of lamb in the basket, then insert basket in unit.
4. Select Zone 1, select ROAST, set temperature to 390°F, and set time to 14 minutes. Press the START/PAUSE button to begin cooking.
5. With 7 minutes remaining, press START/PAUSE to pause the unit. Remove the basket from unit and flip the rack of lamb over. Reinsert basket in unit and press START/PAUSE to resume cooking.
6. When cooking is complete, remove basket from unit. Transfer rack of lamb to a plate. Serve warm.

Lollipop Lamb Chops

|PREP TIME: 15 minutes
|COOK TIME: 18 minutes

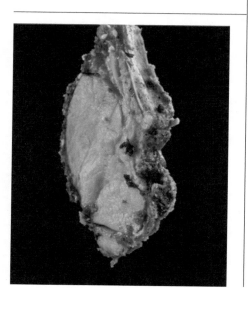

½ small clove garlic
¼ cup packed fresh parsley
¾ cup packed fresh mint
½ tsp. lemon juice
¼ cup grated Parmesan cheese
⅓ cup shelled pistachios
¼ tsp. salt

½ cup olive oil
8 lamb chops (1 rack)
2 tbsps. vegetable oil
Salt and freshly ground black pepper, to taste
1 tbsp. dried rosemary, chopped
1 tbsp. dried thyme

1. Make the pesto by combining the garlic, parsley and mint in a food processor and process until finely chopped. Add the lemon juice, Parmesan cheese, pistachios and salt. Process until all the ingredients have turned into a paste. With the processor running, slowly pour the olive oil in. Scrape the sides of the processor with a spatula and process for another 30 seconds.
2. Rub both sides of the lamb chops with vegetable oil and season with salt, pepper, rosemary and thyme, pressing the herbs into the meat gently with the fingers.
3. Install a crisper plate in both baskets. Place 4 lamb chops in a single layer in each basket.
4. Select Zone 1, select AIR FRY, set temperature to 390°F, and set time to 18 minutes. Select MATCH COOK to match Zone 2 settings to Zone 1. Select START/PAUSE to begin cooking.
5. When the Zone 1 and 2 times reach 8 minutes, press START/PAUSE to pause the unit. Remove the baskets from unit and flip the lamb chops over. Reinsert baskets in unit and press START/PAUSE to resume cooking.
6. When cooking is complete, transfer lamb chops to a plate. Serve the lamb chops with mint pesto drizzled on top.

CHAPTER 6
Pork

Barbecue Pork Ribs with Green Beans

Serves: 4

|PREP TIME: 5 minutes
|COOK TIME: 30 minutes

1 tbsp. barbecue dry rub
1 tsp. mustard
1 tbsp. apple cider vinegar
1 tsp. sesame oil
1 pound (454 g) pork ribs, chopped
1 pound green beans, trimmed and halved
1 tsp. unsalted butter, melted
¼ tsp. garlic powder

1. Combine the dry rub, mustard, apple cider vinegar, and sesame oil, then coat the ribs with this mixture. Refrigerate the ribs for 20 minutes.
2. Mix green beans, butter and garlic powder in a bowl and toss to coat well.
3. Install a crisper plate in both baskets. Place ribs in the Zone 1 basket, then insert basket in unit. Place green beans in the Zone 2 basket, then insert basket in unit.
4. Select Zone 1, select AIR FRY, set temperature to 390°F, and set time to 30 minutes. Select Zone 2, select AIR FRY, set temperature to 390°F, and set time to 15 minutes. Select SMART FINISH. Press the START/PAUSE button to begin cooking.
5. When the Zone 1 and Zone 2 times reach 10 minutes, press START/PAUSE and remove baskets from unit. In Zone 1, flip the rib over. In Zone 2, shake for 10 seconds. Reinsert baskets in unit and press START/PAUSE to resume cooking.
6. When cooking is complete, serve rib with green beans.

Simple Pulled Pork

Serves: 1

|PREP TIME: 5 minutes
|COOK TIME: 22 minutes

2 tbsps. barbecue dry rub
1 pound (454 g) pork tenderloin
⅓ cup heavy cream
1 tsp. butter

1. Massage the dry rub into the tenderloin, coating it well.
2. Install a crisper plate in a basket. Place tenderloin in the basket, then insert basket in unit.
3. Select Zone 1, select AIR FRY, set temperature to 375°F, and set time to 22 minutes. Press the START/PAUSE button to begin cooking.
4. With 5 minutes remaining, press START/PAUSE to pause the unit. Remove the basket from unit and shred with two forks. Add the heavy cream and butter into the basket along with the shredded pork. Reinsert basket in unit and press START/PAUSE to resume cooking.
5. When cooking is complete, remove basket from unit. Transfer shredded pork to a plate. Allow to cool, then serve.

Easy Devils on Horseback

Serves: 12

|PREP TIME: 5 minutes
|COOK TIME: 12 minutes

24 petite pitted prunes (4½ ounces / 128 g)
¼ cup crumbled blue cheese, divided
8 slices center-cut bacon, cut crosswise into thirds

1. Halve the prunes lengthwise, but don't cut them all the way through. Place ½ tsp. of cheese in the center of each prune. Wrap a piece of bacon around each prune and secure the bacon with a toothpick.
2. Install a crisper plate in both baskets. Place half of the prunes in a single layer in each basket.
3. Select Zone 1, select AIR FRY, set temperature to 400°F, and set time to 12 minutes. Select MATCH COOK to match Zone 2 settings to Zone 1. Select START/PAUSE to begin cooking.
4. When the Zone 1 and 2 times reach 6 minutes, press START/PAUSE to pause the unit. Remove the baskets from unit and flip the prunes over. Reinsert baskets in unit and press START/PAUSE to resume cooking.
5. When cooking is complete, transfer prunes to a plate. Serve warm.

Marinated Pork Tenderloin

Serves: 4-6

|PREP TIME: 10 minutes
|COOK TIME: 30 minutes

¼ cup olive oil
¼ cup soy sauce
¼ cup freshly squeezed lemon juice
1 garlic clove, minced
1 tbsp. Dijon mustard
1 tsp. salt
½ tsp. freshly ground black pepper
2 pounds (907 g) pork tenderloin

1. In a large mixing bowl, make the marinade: Mix the olive oil, soy sauce, lemon juice, minced garlic, Dijon mustard, salt, and pepper. Reserve ¼ cup of the marinade.
2. Put the tenderloin in a large bowl and pour the remaining marinade over the meat. Cover and marinate in the refrigerator for about 1 hour.
3. Install a crisper plate in a basket. Place marinated pork tenderloin in the basket, then insert basket in unit.
4. Select Zone 1, select ROAST, set temperature to 375°F, and set time to 30 minutes. Press the START/PAUSE button to begin cooking.
5. With 20 minutes remaining, press START/PAUSE to pause the unit. Remove the basket from unit. Flip the pork over and baste it with half of the reserved marinade.. Reinsert basket in unit and press START/PAUSE to resume cooking.
6. With 10 minutes remaining, press START/PAUSE to pause the unit. Remove the basket from unit. Flip the pork over and baste it with the remaining marinade. Reinsert basket in unit and press START/PAUSE to resume cooking.
7. When cooking is complete, remove basket from unit. Allow to sit 8 minutes to rest before slicing.

Bacon Wrapped Pork with Apple Gravy

Serves: 4

|PREP TIME: 10 minutes
|COOK TIME: 25 minutes

For the Pork:
1 tbsp. Dijon mustard
1 pork tenderloin
3 strips bacon
For the Apple Gravy:
3 tbsps. ghee, divided

1 small shallot, chopped
2 apples
1 tbsp. almond flour
1 cup vegetable broth
½ tsp. Dijon mustard

1. Spread Dijon mustard all over tenderloin and wrap with strips of bacon.
2. Install a crisper plate in a basket. Place wrapped pork in the basket, then insert basket in unit.
3. Select Zone 1, select AIR FRY, set temperature to 375°F, and set time to 20 minutes. Press the START/PAUSE button to begin cooking.
4. With 10 minutes remaining, press START/PAUSE to pause the unit. Remove the basket from unit and flip the pork over. Reinsert basket in unit and press START/PAUSE to resume cooking.
5. To make sauce, heat 1 tbsp. of ghee in a pan and add shallots. Cook for 1 minute.
6. Then add apples, cooking for 4 minutes until softened.
7. Add flour and 2 tbsps. of ghee to make a roux. Add broth and mustard, stirring well to combine.
8. When sauce starts to bubble, add 1 cup of sautéed apples, cooking until sauce thickens.
9. Once pork tenderloin is cooked, remove basket from unit. Allow to sit 8 minutes to rest before slicing.
10. Serve topped with apple gravy.

Five Spice Pork

Serves: 4

|PREP TIME: 15 minutes
|COOK TIME: 15 minutes

1-pound pork belly
2 tbsps. swerve
2 tbsps. dark soy sauce
1 tbsp. Shaoxing (cooking wine)
2 tsps. garlic, minced
2 tsps. ginger, minced
1 tbsp. hoisin sauce
1 tsp. Chinese Five Spice

1. Mix all the ingredients in a bowl and place in the Ziplock bag.
2. Seal the bag, shake it well and refrigerate to marinate for about 1 hour.
3. Remove the pork from the bag.
4. Install a crisper plate in a basket. Place the pork in the basket, then insert basket in unit.
5. Select Zone 1, select AIR FRY, set temperature to 390°F, and set time to 15 minutes. Press the START/PAUSE button to begin cooking.
6. With 7 minutes remaining, press START/PAUSE to pause the unit. Remove the basket from unit and flip the the pork over. Reinsert basket in unit and press START/PAUSE to resume cooking.
7. When cooking is complete, remove basket from unit. Transfer the pork to a plate. Serve warm.

Orange Pork Tenderloin

Serves: 3-4

|PREP TIME: 15 minutes
|COOK TIME: 20 minutes

2 tbsps. coconut sugar
2 tsps. cornstarch
2 tsps. Dijon mustard
½ cup orange juice
½ tsp. soy sauce
2 tsps. grated fresh ginger
¼ cup white wine
Zest of 1 orange

1 pound (454 g) pork tenderloin
Salt and freshly ground black pepper, to taste
Oranges, halved, for garnish
Fresh parsley, for garnish

1. Combine the coconut sugar, cornstarch, Dijon mustard, orange juice, soy sauce, ginger, white wine and orange zest in a small saucepan and bring the mixture to a boil on the stovetop. Lower the heat and simmer while you air fry the pork tenderloin or until the sauce has thickened.
2. Season all sides of the pork tenderloin with salt and freshly ground black pepper.
3. Install a crisper plate in a basket. Place tenderloin in the basket, then insert basket in unit.
4. Select Zone 1, select AIR FRY, set temperature to 375°F, and set time to 20 minutes. Press the START/PAUSE button to begin cooking.
5. With 10 minutes remaining, press START/PAUSE to pause the unit. Remove the basket from unit and flip the tenderloin over, then baste with the sauce. Reinsert basket in unit and press START/PAUSE to resume cooking.
6. When cooking is complete, remove basket from unit. Transfer the tenderloin to a cutting board and let it rest for 5 minutes. Slice the pork at a slight angle and serve immediately with orange halves and fresh parsley.

Pepper Pork Chops

Serves: 2

|PREP TIME: 15 minutes
|COOK TIME: 15 minutes

2 pork chops
1 egg white
¾ cup xanthum gum
½ tsp. sea salt
¼ tsp. freshly ground black pepper
1 oil mister

1. Whisk egg white with salt and black pepper in a bowl and dip the pork chops in it.
2. Cover the bowl and marinate for about 20 minutes.
3. Pour the xanthum gum over both sides of the chops and spray with oil mister.
4. Install a crisper plate in a basket. Place chops in the basket, then insert basket in unit.
5. Select Zone 1, select ROAST, set temperature to 390°F, and set time to 15 minutes. Press the START/PAUSE button to begin cooking.
6. With 7 minutes remaining, press START/PAUSE to pause the unit. Remove the basket from unit and flip the chops over. Reinsert basket in unit and press START/PAUSE to resume cooking.
7. When cooking is complete, remove basket from unit. Transfer chops to a plate. Serve warm.

Garlic Butter Pork Chops

Serves: 4

|PREP TIME: 10 minutes
|COOK TIME: 24 minutes

4 pork chops
1 tbsp. coconut butter
2 tsps. parsley
1 tbsp. coconut oil
2 tsps. garlic, grated
Salt and black pepper, to taste

1. Mix all the seasonings, coconut oil, garlic, butter, and parsley in a bowl and coat the pork chops with it.
2. Cover the chops with foil and refrigerate to marinate for about 1 hour.
3. Install a crisper plate in both baskets. Remove the foil and arrange 2 chops in a single layer in each basket.
4. Select Zone 1, select ROAST, set temperature to 390°F, and set time to 20 minutes. Select MATCH COOK to match Zone 2 settings to Zone 1. Select START/PAUSE to begin cooking.
5. When the Zone 1 and 2 times reach 10 minutes, press START/PAUSE to pause the unit. Remove the baskets from unit and flip the chops over. Reinsert baskets in unit and press START/PAUSE to resume cooking.
6. When cooking is complete, transfer pork chops to a plate. Serve warm.

Citrus Pork Loin Roast

Serves: 8

|PREP TIME: 10 minutes
|COOK TIME: 40 minutes

1 tbsp. lime juice
1 tbsp. orange marmalade
1 tsp. coarse brown mustard
1 tsp. curry powder
1 tsp. dried lemongrass
2 pound (907 g) boneless pork loin roast
Salt and ground black pepper, to taste
Cooking spray

1. Mix the lime juice, marmalade, mustard, curry powder, and lemongrass.
2. Rub mixture all over the surface of the pork loin. Season with salt and pepper.
3. Install a crisper plate in a basket. Place pork roast diagonally in the basket and spray with cooking spray. then insert basket in unit.
4. Select Zone 1, select ROAST, set temperature to 375°F, and set time to 40 minutes. Press the START/PAUSE button to begin cooking.
5. When cooking is complete, remove basket from unit. Wrap roast in foil and let rest for 10 minutes before slicing.

Cheese Crusted Chops

Serves: 6

|PREP TIME: 10 minutes
|COOK TIME: 18 minutes

¼ tsp. pepper
½ tsp. salt
6 thick boneless pork chops
1 cup pork rind crumbs
¼ tsp. chili powder

½ tsp. onion powder
1 tsp. smoked paprika
2 beaten eggs
3 tbsps. grated Parmesan cheese
Cooking spray

1. Rub the pepper and salt on both sides of pork chops.
2. In a food processor, pulse pork rinds into crumbs. Mix crumbs with chili powder, onion powder, and paprika in a bowl.
3. Beat eggs in another bowl.
4. Dip pork chops into eggs then into pork rind crumb mixture.
5. Install a crisper plate in both baskets. Place 3 pork chops in a single layer in each basket. Spritz with cooking spray.
6. Select Zone 1, select AIR FRY, set temperature to 390°F, and set time to 18 minutes. Select MATCH COOK to match Zone 2 settings to Zone 1. Select START/PAUSE to begin cooking.
7. When the Zone 1 and 2 times reach 9 minutes, press START/PAUSE to pause the unit. Remove the baskets from unit and flip the pork chops over. Reinsert baskets in unit and press START/PAUSE to resume cooking.
8. When cooking is complete, transfer pork chops to a plate. Serve warm.

Smoky Flavored Pork Ribs

Serves: 6

|PREP TIME: 10 minutes
|COOK TIME: 18 minutes

1¾ pounds pork ribs
¼ cup honey, divided
¾ cup BBQ sauce
2 tbsps. tomato ketchup
1 tbsp. Worcestershire sauce
1 tbsp. soy sauce
½ tsp. garlic powder
Freshly ground white pepper, to taste

1. Mix 3 tbsps. of honey and remaining ingredients in a large bowl except the ribs.
2. Coat the pork ribs with marinade generously and cover to refrigerate for about 30 minutes.
3. Install a crisper plate in a basket. Place ribs in the basket, then insert basket in unit.
4. Select Zone 1, select AIR FRY, set temperature to 355°F, and set time to 18 minutes. Press the START/PAUSE button to begin cooking.
5. With 8 minutes remaining, press START/PAUSE to pause the unit. Remove the basket from unit and flip the ribs over. Reinsert basket in unit and press START/PAUSE to resume cooking.
6. When cooking is complete, remove basket from unit. Transfer ribs to a plate. Coat with remaining honey and serve hot.

CHAPTER 7
Beef

Herbed Beef

|PREP TIME: 5 minutes
|COOK TIME: 22 minutes

1 tsp. dried dill
1 tsp. dried thyme
1 tsp. garlic powder
2 pounds (907 g) beef steak
3 tbsps. butter

1. Combine the dill, thyme, and garlic powder in a small bowl, and massage into the steak.
2. Install a crisper plate in a basket. Place the steak in the basket, then insert basket in unit.
3. Select Zone 1, select AIR FRY, set temperature to 390°F, and set time to 22 minutes. Press the START/PAUSE button to begin cooking.
4. With 10 minutes remaining, press START/PAUSE to pause the unit. Remove the basket from unit and flip the steak over. Reinsert basket in unit and press START/PAUSE to resume cooking.
5. With 2 minutes remaining, press START/PAUSE to pause the unit. Remove the basket from unit and shred the steak. Return to the basket and add the butter. Reinsert basket in unit and reduce the temperature to 365°F, press START/PAUSE to resume cooking.
6. When cooking is complete, remove basket from unit. Transfer the steak to a plate. Serve warm.

Bacon Wrapped Filet Mignon

|PREP TIME: 15 minutes
|COOK TIME: 15 minutes

2 bacon slices
2 (6-ounces) filet mignon steaks
Salt and black pepper, to taste
1 tsp. avocado oil

1. Wrap each mignon steak with 1 bacon slice and secure with a toothpick.
2. Season the steak generously with salt and black pepper and coat with avocado oil.
3. Install a crisper plate in a basket. Place the steak in the basket, then insert basket in unit.
4. Select Zone 1, select AIR FRY, set temperature to 375°F, and set time to 15 minutes. Press the START/PAUSE button to begin cooking.
5. With 7 minutes remaining, press START/PAUSE to pause the unit. Remove the basket from unit and flip the steak over. Reinsert basket in unit and press START/PAUSE to resume cooking.
6. When cooking is complete, remove basket from unit. Transfer the steak to a plate and cut into desired size slices to serve.

Simple Beef Bratwursts

Serves: 4

|PREP TIME: 5 minutes
|COOK TIME: 15 minutes

4 (3-ounce / 85-g) beef bratwursts

1. Install a crisper plate in a basket. Place the beef bratwursts in the basket, then insert basket in unit.
2. Select Zone 1, select AIR FRY, set temperature to 375°F, and set time to 15 minutes. Press the START/PAUSE button to begin cooking.
3. With 8 minutes remaining, press START/PAUSE to pause the unit. Remove the basket from unit and flip the beef bratwursts over. Reinsert basket in unit and press START/PAUSE to resume cooking.
4. When cooking is complete, remove basket from unit. Transfer the beef bratwursts to a plate. Serve hot.

Easy Rib Steak

Serves: 4

|PREP TIME: 10 minutes
|COOK TIME: 18 minutes

2 lbs. rib steak
2 cup steak rub
1 tbsp. olive oil

1. Rub the steak generously with steak rub, salt and black pepper, and coat with olive oil.
2. Install a crisper plate in a basket. Place the steak in the basket, then insert basket in unit.
3. Select Zone 1, select ROAST, set temperature to 390°F, and set time to 18 minutes. Press the START/PAUSE button to begin cooking.
4. With 9 minutes remaining, press START/PAUSE to pause the unit. Remove the basket from unit and flip the steak over. Reinsert basket in unit and press START/PAUSE to resume cooking.
5. When cooking is complete, remove basket from unit. Transfer the steak to a plate and cut into desired size slices to serve.

(Note: To prepare the Steak Rub - 2 tbsps. fresh cracked black pepper, 2 tbsps. kosher salt, 2 tbsps. paprika, 1 tbsp. crushed red pepper flakes, 1 tbsp. crushed coriander seeds (not ground), 1 tbsp. garlic powder, 1 tbsp. onion powder, 2 tsps. cayenne pepper. Mix all ingredients in a medium bowl and stir well to combine.)

Buttered Rib Eye Steak

|PREP TIME: 20 minutes
|COOK TIME: 15 minutes

½ cup unsalted butter, softened
2 tbsps. fresh parsley, chopped
2 (8-ounces) rib eye steaks
2 tsps. garlic, minced
1 tsp. Worcestershire sauce
1 tbsp. olive oil
Salt and black pepper, to taste

1. Mix the butter, parsley, garlic, Worcestershire sauce, and salt in a bowl.
2. Place the butter mixture onto a parchment paper, roll into a log and refrigerate for about 3 hours.
3. Rub the steak generously with olive oil, salt and black pepper.
4. Install a crisper plate in a basket. Place the steaks in the basket, then insert basket in unit.
5. Select Zone 1, select AIR FRY, set temperature to 390°F, and set time to 15 minutes. Press the START/PAUSE button to begin cooking.
6. With 8 minutes remaining, press START/PAUSE to pause the unit. Remove the basket from unit and flip the steaks over. Reinsert basket in unit and press START/PAUSE to resume cooking.
7. When cooking is complete, remove basket from unit. Transfer the steaks to a plate and cut into desired size slices. Cut the butter log into slices and top over the steak to serve.

Easy Beef Schnitzel

|PREP TIME: 5 minutes
|COOK TIME: 12 minutes

½ cup friendly bread crumbs
2 tbsps. olive oil
Pepper and salt, to taste
1 egg, beaten
1 thin beef schnitzel

1. In a shallow dish, combine the bread crumbs, oil, pepper, and salt.
2. In a second shallow dish, place the beaten egg.
3. Dredge the schnitzel in the egg before rolling it in the bread crumbs.
4. Install a crisper plate in a basket. Place the coated schnitzel in the basket, then insert basket in unit.
5. Select Zone 1, select AIR FRY, set temperature to 350°F, and set time to 12 minutes. Press the START/PAUSE button to begin cooking.
6. With 6 minutes remaining, press START/PAUSE to pause the unit. Remove the basket from unit and flip the schnitzel over. Reinsert basket in unit and press START/PAUSE to resume cooking.
7. When cooking is complete, remove basket from unit. Transfer the schnitzel to a plate. Serve immediately.

Air Fried Beef Ribs

Serves: 4

|PREP TIME: 20 minutes
|COOK TIME: 14 minutes

1 pound (454 g) meaty beef ribs, rinsed and drained
3 tbsps. apple cider vinegar
1 cup coriander, finely chopped
1 tbsp. fresh basil leaves, chopped
2 garlic cloves, finely chopped
1 chipotle powder
1 tsp. fennel seeds
1 tsp. hot paprika
Kosher salt and black pepper, to taste
½ cup vegetable oil

1. Coat the ribs with the remaining ingredients and refrigerate for at least 3 hours.
2. Install a crisper plate in a basket. Separate the ribs from the marinade and put in the basket, then insert basket in unit.
3. Select Zone 1, select AIR FRY, set temperature to 360°F, and set time to 14 minutes. Press the START/PAUSE button to begin cooking.
4. With 7 minutes remaining, press START/PAUSE to pause the unit. Remove the basket from unit and flip the ribs over. Reinsert basket in unit and press START/PAUSE to resume cooking.
5. When cooking is complete, remove basket from unit. Transfer the ribs to a plate. Pour the remaining marinade over the ribs before serving.

Swedish Beef Meatballs

Serves: 8

|PREP TIME: 10 minutes
|COOK TIME: 15 minutes

1 pound (454 g) ground beef
1 egg, beaten
2 carrots, shredded
2 whole wheat bread slices, crumbled
1 small onion, minced
½ tsp. garlic salt
Pepper and salt, to taste
1 cup tomato sauce
2 cups pasta sauce

1. In a bowl, combine the ground beef, egg, carrots, crumbled bread, onion, garlic salt, pepper and salt.
2. Divide the mixture into equal amounts and shape each one into a small meatball.
3. Install a crisper plate in a basket. Place meatballs in the basket, then insert basket in unit.
4. Select Zone 1, select AIR FRY, set temperature to 390°F, and set time to 10 minutes. Press the START/PAUSE button to begin cooking.
5. When cooking is complete, remove basket from unit. Transfer the meatballs to an oven-safe dish and top with the tomato sauce and pasta sauce.
6. Set the dish into the basket and allow to air fry at 320ºF for 5 more minutes. Serve hot.

Veggie Stuffed Beef Rolls

Serves: 6

PREP TIME: 20 minutes
COOK TIME: 16 minutes

2 pounds beef flank steak, pounded to ⅛-inch thickness
6 Provolone cheese slices
3-ounce roasted red bell peppers
¾ cup fresh baby spinach
3 tbsps. prepared pesto
Salt and black pepper, to taste

1. Place the steak onto a smooth surface and spread evenly with pesto.
2. Top with the cheese slices, red peppers and spinach.
3. Roll up the steak tightly around the filling and secure with the toothpicks.
4. Install a crisper plate in a basket. Place roll in the basket, then insert basket in unit.
5. Select Zone 1, select ROAST, set temperature to 390°F, and set time to 16 minutes. Press the START/PAUSE button to begin cooking.
6. With 8 minutes remaining, press START/PAUSE to pause the unit. Remove the basket from unit and flip the roll over. Reinsert basket in unit and press START/PAUSE to resume cooking.
7. When cooking is complete, remove basket from unit. Transfer roll to a plate. Serve warm.

Beef Steak Fingers

Serves: 4

PREP TIME: 5 minutes
COOK TIME: 10 minutes

4 small beef cube steaks
Salt and ground black pepper, to taste
½ cup whole wheat flour
Cooking spray

1. Cut cube steaks into 1-inch-wide strips.
2. Sprinkle lightly with salt and pepper to taste.
3. Roll in flour to coat all sides.
4. Install a crisper plate in both baskets. Place half of steak strips in a single layer in each basket. Spritz steak strips with cooking spray.
5. Select Zone 1, select AIR FRY, set temperature to 390°F, and set time to 10 minutes. Select MATCH COOK to match Zone 2 settings to Zone 1. Select START/PAUSE to begin cooking.
6. When the Zone 1 and 2 times reach 5 minutes, press START/PAUSE to pause the unit. Remove the baskets from unit and flip the steak strips over. Spritz with cooking spray. Reinsert baskets in unit and press START/PAUSE to resume cooking.
7. When cooking is complete, steak fingers should be crispy outside with no red juices inside. Transfer to a plate and serve warm.

Classic Spring Rolls

Serves: 20

|PREP TIME: 10 minutes
|COOK TIME: 8 minutes

⅓ cup noodles
1 cup ground beef
1 tsp. soy sauce
1 cup fresh mix vegetables
3 garlic cloves, minced
1 small onion, diced
1 tbsp. sesame oil
1 packet spring roll sheets
2 tbsps. cold water

1. Cook the noodle in enough hot water to soften them up, drain them and snip them to make them shorter.
2. In a frying pan over medium heat, cook the beef, soy sauce, mixed vegetables, garlic, and onion in sesame oil until the beef is cooked through. Take the pan off the heat and throw in the noodles. Mix well to incorporate everything.
3. Unroll a spring roll sheet and lay it flat. Scatter the filling diagonally across it and roll it up, brushing the edges lightly with water to act as an adhesive. Repeat until you have used up all the sheets and the filling.
4. Coat each spring roll with a light brushing of oil.
5. Install a crisper plate in both baskets. Place half of the spring rolls in a single layer in each basket.
6. Select Zone 1, select AIR FRY, set temperature to 350°F, and set time to 8 minutes. Select MATCH COOK to match Zone 2 settings to Zone 1. Select START/PAUSE to begin cooking.
7. When the Zone 1 and 2 times reach 4 minutes, press START/PAUSE to pause the unit. Remove the baskets from unit and flip the spring rolls over. Reinsert baskets in unit and press START/PAUSE to resume cooking.
8. When cooking is complete, transfer spring rolls to a plate. Serve hot.

Mozzarella Beef Brisket

Serves: 6

|PREP TIME: 5 minutes
|COOK TIME: 25 minutes

12 ounces (340 g) beef brisket
2 tsps. Italian herbs
2 tsps. olive oil
1 onion, sliced
7 ounces (198 g) Mozzarella cheese, sliced

1. Cut up the brisket into four equal slices and season with the Italian herbs.
2. Drizzle the slices of beef with olive oil.
3. Install a crisper plate in a basket. Place the brisket slices in the basket along with the onion, then insert basket in unit.
4. Select Zone 1, select AIR FRY, set temperature to 365°F, and set time to 25 minutes. Press the START/PAUSE button to begin cooking.
5. With 5 minutes remaining, press START/PAUSE to pause the unit. Remove the basket from unit and put a piece of Mozzarella on top of each piece of brisket. Reinsert basket in unit and press START/PAUSE to resume cooking.
6. When cooking is complete, remove basket from unit. Transfer brisket slices to a plate. Serve warm.

CHAPTER 8
Fish and Seafood

Spicy Shrimps

Serves: 3

|PREP TIME: 15 minutes
|COOK TIME: 8 minutes

1 pound shrimps, peeled and deveined
2 tbsps. olive oil
1 tsp. old bay seasoning
½ tsp. red chili flakes
½ tsp. smoked paprika
½ tsp. cayenne pepper
Salt, as required

1. Mix shrimp with olive oil and other seasonings in a large bowl.
2. Install a crisper plate in a basket. Place shrimp in the basket, then insert basket in unit.
3. Select Zone 1, select AIR FRY, set temperature to 390°F, and set time to 8 minutes. Press the START/PAUSE button to begin cooking.
4. With 4 minutes remaining, press START/PAUSE to pause the unit. Remove the basket from unit and shake for 10 seconds. Reinsert basket in unit and press START/PAUSE to resume cooking.
5. When cooking is complete, remove basket from unit. Transfer shrimp to a plate. Serve warm.

Simple Salmon

Serves: 2

|PREP TIME: 5 minutes
|COOK TIME: 10 minutes

2 (6-ounces) salmon fillets
Salt and black pepper, as required
1 tbsp. olive oil

1. Season each salmon fillet with salt and black pepper and drizzle with olive oil.
2. Install a crisper plate in a basket. Place salmon in the basket, then insert basket in unit.
3. Select Zone 1, select AIR FRY, set temperature to 400°F, and set time to 10 minutes. Press the START/PAUSE button to begin cooking.
4. When cooking is complete, remove basket from unit. Transfer salmon to a plate. Serve warm.

Roasted Cod with Broccoli

|PREP TIME: 5 minutes
|COOK TIME: 17 minutes

1 tbsp. reduced-sodium soy sauce
2 tsps. honey
Cooking spray
2 (6-ounces) fresh cod fillets
1 tsp. sesame seeds
4 cups fresh broccoli florets
2 tbsps. butter, melted
Salt and black pepper, to taste

1. In a small bowl, combine the soy sauce and honey.
2. Brush the cod fillets with the soy mixture, and sprinkle sesame seeds on top.
3. Mix broccoli, butter, salt, and black pepper in a bowl and toss to coat well.
4. Install a crisper plate in both baskets. Place cod fillets in the Zone 1 basket, then insert basket in unit. Place broccoli in the Zone 2 basket, then insert basket in unit.
5. Select Zone 1, select AIR FRY, set temperature to 390°F, and set time to 15 minutes. Select Zone 2, select ROAST, set temperature to 390°F, and set time to 17 minutes. Select SMART FINISH. Press the START/PAUSE button to begin cooking.
6. When cooking is complete, serve fillets with broccoli florets.

Creamy Tuna Cakes

|PREP TIME: 15 minutes
|COOK TIME: 12 minutes

Cooking spray
2 (6-ounces) cans tuna, drained
1½ tbsps. almond flour
1½ tbsps. mayonnaise
1 tbsp. fresh lemon juice
1 tsp. dried dill
1 tsp. garlic powder
½ tsp. onion powder
Pinch of salt and ground black pepper

1. Mix the tuna, mayonnaise, almond flour, lemon juice, dill, and spices in a large bowl.
2. Make 4 equal-sized patties from the mixture.
3. Install a crisper plate in a basket and spray with cooking spray. Place patties in the basket, then insert basket in unit.
4. Select Zone 1, select BAKE, set temperature to 390°F, and set time to 12 minutes. Press the START/PAUSE button to begin cooking.
5. With 6 minutes remaining, press START/PAUSE to pause the unit. Remove the basket from unit and flip the patties over. Reinsert basket in unit and press START/PAUSE to resume cooking.
6. When cooking is complete, remove basket from unit. Transfer tuna cakes to a plate. Serve warm.

Mahi Mahi with Green Beans

Serves: 4

|PREP TIME: 15 minutes
|COOK TIME: 15 minutes

5 cups green beans
2 tbsps. fresh dill, chopped
4 (6-ounces) Mahi Mahi fillets
1 tbsp. avocado oil
Salt, as required
2 garlic cloves, minced
2 tbsps. fresh lemon juice
1 tbsp. olive oil

1. Combine garlic, dill, lemon juice, salt and olive oil in a bowl. Coat Mahi Mahi in this garlic mixture.
2. Mix the green beans, avocado oil and salt in a large bowl.
3. Install a crisper plate in both baskets. Place Mahi Mahi in the Zone 1 basket, then insert basket in unit. Place green beans in the Zone 2 basket, then insert basket in unit.
4. Select Zone 1, select AIR FRY, set temperature to 390°F, and set time to 15 minutes. Select MATCH COOK to match Zone 2 settings to Zone 1. Press the START/PAUSE button to begin cooking.
5. When cooking is complete, serve Mahi Mahi immediately with green beans.

Breaded Hake

Serves: 2

|PREP TIME: 15 minutes
|COOK TIME: 15 minutes

1 egg
4 ounces breadcrumbs
4 (6-ounces) hake fillets
1 lemon, cut into wedges
2 tbsps. vegetable oil

1. Whisk the egg in a shallow bowl and mix breadcrumbs and oil in another bowl.
2. Dip hake fillets into the whisked egg and then, dredge in the bread-crumb mixture.
3. Install a crisper plate in both baskets. Place 2 hake fillets in a single layer in each basket.
4. Select Zone 1, select AIR FRY, set temperature to 390°F, and set time to 15 minutes. Select MATCH COOK to match Zone 2 settings to Zone 1. Select START/PAUSE to begin cooking.
5. When the Zone 1 and 2 times reach 8 minutes, press START/PAUSE to pause the unit. Remove the baskets from unit and flip the hake fillets over. Lightly spray with the cooking spray. Reinsert baskets in unit and press START/PAUSE to resume cooking.
6. When cooking is complete, transfer hake fillets to a plate. Serve with lemon wedges.

Lemon Garlic Shrimps

Serves: 2

|PREP TIME: 15 minutes
|COOK TIME: 10 minutes

¾ pound medium shrimp, peeled and deveined
1½ tbsps. fresh lemon juice
1 tbsp. olive oil
1 tsp. lemon pepper
¼ tsp. paprika
¼ tsp. garlic powder

1. Mix lemon juice, olive oil, lemon pepper, paprika and garlic powder in a large bowl.
2. Stir in the shrimp and toss until well combined.
3. Install a crisper plate in a basket. Place shrimp in the basket, then insert basket in unit.
4. Select Zone 1, select AIR FRY, set temperature to 390°F, and set time to 10 minutes. Press the START/PAUSE button to begin cooking.
5. With 5 minutes remaining, press START/PAUSE to pause the unit. Remove the basket from unit and shake the shrimp for 10 seconds. Reinsert basket in unit and press START/PAUSE to resume cooking.
6. When cooking is complete, remove basket from unit. Transfer shrimp to a plate. Serve warm.

Cajun Coated Catfish

Serves: 4

|PREP TIME: 15 minutes
|COOK TIME: 12 minutes

2 tbsps. cornmeal polenta
2 (6-ounces) catfish fillets
2 tsps. Cajun seasoning
½ tsp. paprika
½ tsp. garlic powder
Salt, as required
1 tbsp. olive oil

1. Mix the cornmeal, Cajun seasoning, paprika, garlic powder, and salt in a bowl.
2. Stir in the catfish fillets and coat evenly with the mixture.
3. Drizzle each fillet with olive oil.
4. Install a crisper plate in a basket. Place catfish fillets in the basket, then insert basket in unit.
5. Select Zone 1, select AIR FRY, set temperature to 400°F, and set time to 12 minutes. Press the START/PAUSE button to begin cooking.
6. With 5 minutes remaining, press START/PAUSE to pause the unit. Remove the basket from unit and flip the catfish fillets over. Reinsert basket in unit and press START/PAUSE to resume cooking.
7. When cooking is complete, remove basket from unit. Transfer catfish fillets to a plate. Serve warm.

Glazed Halibut Steak

Serves: 4

|PREP TIME: 30 minutes
|COOK TIME: 12 minutes

cooking spray
1 pound haddock steak
1 garlic clove, minced
¼ tsp. fresh ginger, grated finely
½ cup low-sodium soy sauce
¼ cup fresh orange juice

2 tbsps. lime juice
½ cup cooking wine
¼ cup sugar
¼ tsp. red pepper flakes, crushed

1. Put all the ingredients except haddock steak in a pan and bring to a boil.
2. Cook for about 4 minutes, stirring continuously and remove from the heat.
3. Put the haddock steak and half of the marinade in a resealable bag and shake well.
4. Refrigerate for about 1 hour and reserve the remaining marinade.
5. Install a crisper plate in both baskets and spray with cooking spray. Place half of the haddock steaks in a single layer in each basket.
6. Select Zone 1, select AIR FRY, set temperature to 390°F, and set time to 12 minutes. Select MATCH COOK to match Zone 2 settings to Zone 1. Select START/PAUSE to begin cooking.
7. When the Zone 1 and 2 times reach 6 minutes, press START/PAUSE to pause the unit. Remove the baskets from unit and flip the haddock steaks over. Reinsert baskets in unit and press START/PAUSE to resume cooking.
8. When cooking is complete, transfer haddock steaks to a plate. Coat with the remaining glaze and serve hot.

Sweet and Sour Glazed Cod

Serves: 2

|PREP TIME: 20 minutes
|COOK TIME: 12 minutes

1 tsp. water
4 (3½-ounces) cod fillets
⅓ cup soy sauce
⅓ cup honey
3 tsps. rice wine vinegar

1. Mix the soy sauce, honey, vinegar and water in a small bowl.
2. Reserve about half of the mixture in another bowl.
3. Stir the cod fillets in the remaining mixture until well coated.
4. Cover and refrigerate to marinate for about 3 hours.
5. Install a crisper plate in a basket. Place cod fillets in the basket, then insert basket in unit.
6. Select Zone 1, select AIR FRY, set temperature to 390°F, and set time to 12 minutes. Press the START/PAUSE button to begin cooking.
7. With 6 minutes remaining, press START/PAUSE to pause the unit. Remove the basket from unit and flip the fish over. Reinsert basket in unit and press START/PAUSE to resume cooking.
8. When cooking is complete, remove basket from unit. Transfer cod fillets to a plate. Coat with the reserved marinade and serve hot.

Crispy Cod Sticks

Serves: 2

|PREP TIME: 20 minutes
|COOK TIME: 10 minutes

3 (4-ounces) skinless cod fillets, cut into rectangular pieces
¾ cup flour
4 eggs
1 green chili, finely chopped
2 garlic cloves, minced
2 tsps. light soy sauce
Salt and ground black pepper, to taste

1. Place flour in a shallow dish and whisk the eggs, garlic, green chili, soy sauce, salt, and black pepper in a second dish.
2. Coat the cod fillets evenly in flour and dip in the egg mixture.
3. Install a crisper plate in a basket. Place cod pieces in the basket, then insert basket in unit.
4. Select Zone 1, select AIR FRY, set temperature to 390°F, and set time to 10 minutes. Press the START/PAUSE button to begin cooking.
5. When cooking is complete, remove basket from unit. Transfer cod pieces to a plate. Serve warm.

Tuna Patty Sliders

Serves: 4

|PREP TIME: 15 minutes
|COOK TIME: 15 minutes

3 (5-ounce / 142-g) cans tuna, packed in water
⅔ cup whole-wheat panko bread crumbs
⅓ cup shredded Parmesan cheese
1 tbsp. sriracha
¾ tsp. black pepper
10 whole-wheat slider buns
Cooking spray

1. In a medium bowl combine the tuna, bread crumbs, Parmesan cheese, sriracha, and black pepper and stir to combine.
2. Form the mixture into 10 patties.
3. Install a crisper plate in both baskets. Place 5 patties in a single layer in each basket. Spray the patties lightly with cooking spray.
4. Select Zone 1, select AIR FRY, set temperature to 390°F, and set time to 15 minutes. Select MATCH COOK to match Zone 2 settings to Zone 1. Select START/PAUSE to begin cooking.
5. When the Zone 1 and 2 times reach 8 minutes, press START/PAUSE to pause the unit. Remove the baskets from unit and flip the patties over. Lightly spray with the cooking spray. Reinsert baskets in unit and press START/PAUSE to resume cooking.
6. When cooking is complete, transfer patties to a plate. Serve warm.

CHAPTER 9
Snack

Mozzarella Arancini

|PREP TIME: 5 minutes
|COOK TIME: 12 minutes

2 cups cooked rice, cooled
2 eggs, beaten
1½ cups panko bread crumbs, divided
½ cup grated Parmesan cheese
2 tbsps. minced fresh basil
16 ¾-inch cubes Mozzarella cheese
2 tbsps. olive oil

1. In a medium bowl, combine the rice, eggs, ½ cup of the bread crumbs, Parmesan cheese, and basil. Form this mixture into 16 1½-inch balls.
2. Poke a hole in each of the balls with your finger and insert a Mozzarella cube. Form the rice mixture firmly around the cheese.
3. On a shallow plate, combine the remaining 1 cup of the bread crumbs with the olive oil and mix well. Roll the rice balls in the bread crumbs to coat.
4. Install a crisper plate in both baskets. Place half of the arancinis in a single layer in each basket.
5. Select Zone 1, select AIR FRY, set temperature to 360°F, and set time to 12 minutes. Select MATCH COOK to match Zone 2 settings to Zone 1. Select START/PAUSE to begin cooking, until golden brown.
6. Serve hot.

Spicy Kale Chips

|PREP TIME: 5 minutes
|COOK TIME: 15 minutes

5 cups kale, large stems removed and chopped
2 tsps. canola oil
¼ tsp. smoked paprika
¼ tsp. kosher salt
Cooking spray

1. In a large bowl, toss the kale, canola oil, smoked paprika, and kosher salt.
2. Install a crisper plate in both baskets. Place half the kale in each basket. Spray with cooking spray.
3. Select Zone 1, select AIR FRY, set temperature to 390°F, and set time to 15 minutes. Select MATCH COOK to match Zone 2 settings to Zone 1. Select START/PAUSE to begin cooking.
4. When the Zone 1 and 2 times reach 8 minutes, press START/PAUSE to pause the unit. Remove the baskets from unit and shake for 10 seconds. Reinsert baskets in unit and press START/PAUSE to resume cooking.
5. When cooking is complete, transfer kale to a plate and allow to cool on a wire rack for 3 to 5 minutes before serving.

Herbed Pita Chips

|PREP TIME: 5 minutes
|COOK TIME: 6 minutes

¼ tsp. dried basil
¼ tsp. marjoram
¼ tsp. ground oregano
¼ tsp. garlic powder
¼ tsp. ground thyme
¼ tsp. salt
2 whole grain 6-inch pitas
Cooking spray

1. Mix all the seasonings together.
2. Cut each pita half into 4 wedges. Break apart wedges at the fold.
3. Mist one side of pita wedges with oil. Sprinkle with half of seasoning mix.
4. Turn pita wedges over, mist the other side with oil, and sprinkle with remaining seasonings.
5. Install a crisper plate in a basket. Place pita wedges in the basket, then insert basket in unit.
6. Select Zone 1, select AIR FRY, set temperature to 330°F, and set time to 6 minutes. Press the START/PAUSE button to begin cooking, shaking every 2 minutes.
7. When cooking is complete, remove basket from unit. Serve hot.

Cajun Zucchini Chips

|PREP TIME: 5 minutes
|COOK TIME: 15-16 minutes

2 large zucchinis, cut into ⅛-inch-thick slices
2 tsps. Cajun seasoning
Cooking spray

1. Put the zucchini slices in a medium bowl and spray them generously with cooking spray.
2. Sprinkle the Cajun seasoning over the zucchini and stir to make sure they are evenly coated with oil and seasoning.
3. Install a crisper plate in both baskets and spray lightly with cooking spray. Place half of the slices in a single layer in each basket.
4. Select Zone 1, select AIR FRY, set temperature to 390°F, and set time to 25 minutes. Select MATCH COOK to match Zone 2 settings to Zone 1. Select START/PAUSE to begin cooking.
5. When the Zone 1 and 2 times reach 12 minutes, press START/PAUSE to pause the unit. Remove the baskets from unit and flip the zucchini slices over. Reinsert baskets in unit and press START/PAUSE to resume cooking.
6. When cooking is complete, transfer zucchini slices to a plate. Serve warm.

Crispy Cajun Dill Pickle Chips

Makes 16 slices

|PREP TIME: 5 minutes
|COOK TIME: 7 minutes

¼ cup all-purpose flour
½ cup panko bread crumbs
1 large egg, beaten
2 tsps. Cajun seasoning
2 large dill pickles, sliced into 8 rounds each
Cooking spray

1. Place the all-purpose flour, panko bread crumbs, and egg into 3 separate shallow bowls, then stir the Cajun seasoning into the flour.
2. Dredge each pickle chip in the flour mixture, then the egg, and finally the bread crumbs. Shake off any excess, then place each coated pickle chip on a plate.
3. Install a crisper plate in both baskets. Place 8 pickle chips in a single layer in each basket. Spray with cooking spray.
4. Select Zone 1, select AIR FRY, set temperature to 390°F, and set time to 7 minutes. Select MATCH COOK to match Zone 2 settings to Zone 1. Select START/PAUSE to begin cooking.
5. When the Zone 1 and 2 times reach 8 minutes, press START/PAUSE to pause the unit. Remove the baskets from unit and flip the pickle chips over. Reinsert baskets in unit and press START/PAUSE to resume cooking.
6. When cooking is complete, transfer pickle chips to a plate and allow to slightly cool on a wire rack before serving.

Spinach and Crab Meat Cups

Makes 30 cups

|PREP TIME: 10 minutes
|COOK TIME: 7 minutes

1 (6-ounce / 170-g) can crab meat, drained to yield ⅓ cup meat
¼ cup frozen spinach, thawed, drained, and chopped
1 clove garlic, minced
½ cup grated Parmesan cheese
3 tbsps. plain yogurt
¼ tsp. lemon juice
½ tsp. Worcestershire sauce
30 mini frozen phyllo shells, thawed
Cooking spray

1. Remove any bits of shell that might remain in the crab meat.
2. Mix the crab meat, spinach, garlic, and cheese together.
3. Stir in the yogurt, lemon juice, and Worcestershire sauce and mix well.
4. Spoon a tsp. of filling into each phyllo shell.
5. Install a crisper plate in both baskets. Place half the shells in each basket. Spray with cooking spray.
6. Select Zone 1, select BAKE, set temperature to 390°F, and set time to 7 minutes. Select MATCH COOK to match Zone 2 settings to Zone 1. Select START/PAUSE to begin cooking.
7. When cooking is complete, transfer shells to a plate. Serve warm.

Simple and Easy Croutons

Serves: 4

|PREP TIME: 5 minutes
|COOK TIME: 10 minutes

2 slices friendly bread
1 tbsp. olive oil
Hot soup, for serving

1. Cut the slices of bread into medium-size chunks.
2. Install a crisper plate in a basket and brush with the oil. Place the bread chunks in the basket, then insert basket in unit.
3. Select Zone 1, select AIR FRY, set temperature to 390°F, and set time to 10 minutes. Press the START/PAUSE button to begin cooking.
4. With 5 minutes remaining, press START/PAUSE to pause the unit. Remove the basket from unit and shake for 10 seconds. Reinsert basket in unit and press START/PAUSE to resume cooking.
5. When cooking is complete, remove basket from unit. Transfer bread chunks to a plate. Serve with hot soup.

Lemony Chicken Drumsticks with Tortilla Chips

Serves: 2

|PREP TIME: 5 minutes
|COOK TIME: 30 minutes

2 tsps. freshly ground coarse black pepper
1 tsp. baking powder
½ tsp. garlic powder
4 chicken drumsticks (4 ounces / 113 g each)
Kosher salt, to taste
1 lemon
2 corn tortillas, sliced the corn tortillas into triangles
1 tbsp. olive oil

1. In a small bowl, stir together the pepper, baking powder, and garlic powder. Place the drumsticks on a plate and sprinkle evenly with the baking powder mixture, turning the drumsticks so they're well coated. Let the drumsticks stand in the refrigerator for at least 1 hour or up to overnight.
2. Coat tortillas pieces with a light brushing of olive oil.
3. Install a crisper plate in both baskets. Sprinkle the drumsticks with salt and arrange in the Zone 1 basket, standing them bone-end up and leaning against the wall of the air fryer basket, then insert basket in unit. Place tortillas pieces in the Zone 2 basket, then insert basket in unit.
4. Select Zone 1, select AIR FRY, set temperature to 375°F, and set time to 30 minutes. Select Zone 2, select AIR FRY, set temperature to 390°F, and set time to 6 minutes. Select SMART FINISH. Press the START/PAUSE button to begin cooking.
5. When cooking is complete, transfer the drumsticks and tortillas pieces to a serving platter. Finely grate the zest of the lemon over the drumsticks while they're hot. Cut the lemon into wedges and serve warm.

Bacon-Wrapped Shrimp and Jalapeño

Serves: 8

|PREP TIME: 20 minutes
|COOK TIME: 26 minutes

24 large shrimp, peeled and deveined, about ¾ pound (340 g)
5 tbsps. barbecue sauce, divided
12 strips bacon, cut in half
24 small pickled jalapeño slices

1. Toss together the shrimp and 3 tbsps. of the barbecue sauce. Let stand for 15 minutes. Soak 24 wooden toothpicks in water for 10 minutes. Wrap 1 piece bacon around the shrimp and jalapeño slice, then secure with a toothpick.
2. Install a crisper plate in both baskets. Place half of the shrimp in a single layer in each basket.
3. Select Zone 1, select AIR FRY, set temperature to 350°F, and set time to 15 minutes. Select MATCH COOK to match Zone 2 settings to Zone 1. Select START/PAUSE to begin cooking.
4. When the Zone 1 and 2 times reach 5 minutes, press START/PAUSE to pause the unit. Remove the baskets from unit and flip the shrimp over. Reinsert baskets in unit and press START/PAUSE to resume cooking.
5. When cooking is complete, transfer shrimp to a plate. Brush with the remaining barbecue sauce and serve.

Baked Halloumi with Greek Salsa

Serves: 4

|PREP TIME: 15 minutes
|COOK TIME: 6 minutes

For the Salsa:
1 small shallot, finely diced
3 garlic cloves, minced
2 tbsps. fresh lemon juice
2 tbsps. extra-virgin olive oil
1 tsp. freshly cracked black pepper
Pinch of kosher salt
½ cup finely diced English cucumber
1 plum tomato, deseeded and finely diced
2 tsps. chopped fresh parsley
1 tsp. snipped fresh dill
1 tsp. snipped fresh oregano
For the Cheese:
8 ounces (227 g) Halloumi cheese, sliced into ½-inch-thick pieces
1 tbsp. extra-virgin olive oil

1. For the salsa: Combine the shallot, garlic, lemon juice, olive oil, pepper, and salt in a medium bowl. Add the cucumber, tomato, parsley, dill, and oregano. Toss gently to combine; set aside.
2. For the cheese: Place the cheese slices in a medium bowl. Drizzle with the olive oil. Toss gently to coat.
3. Install a crisper plate in a basket. Place the cheese in the basket, then insert basket in unit.
4. Select Zone 1, select BAKE, set temperature to 375°F, and set time to 6 minutes. Press the START/PAUSE button to begin cooking.
5. When cooking is complete, remove basket from unit. Divide the cheese among four serving plates. Top with the salsa and serve immediately.

Veggie Salmon Nachos

Serves: 6

|PREP TIME: 10 minutes
|COOK TIME: 12 minutes

2 ounces (57 g) baked no-salt corn tortilla chips
1 (5-ounce / 142-g) baked salmon fillet, flaked
½ cup canned low-sodium black beans, rinsed and drained
1 red bell pepper, chopped
½ cup grated carrot
1 jalapeño pepper, minced
⅓ cup shredded low-sodium low-fat Swiss cheese
1 tomato, chopped

1. In a 7 x 5-inch baking pan, layer the tortilla chips. Top with the salmon, black beans, red bell pepper, carrot, jalapeño, and Swiss cheese.
2. Install a crisper plate in a basket. Place baking pan in the basket, then insert basket in unit.
3. Select Zone 1, select BAKE, set temperature to 360°F, and set time to 12 minutes. Press the START/PAUSE button to begin cooking, until the cheese is melted and starts to brown.
4. When cooking is complete, top with the tomato and serve.

Poutine with Waffle Fries

Serves: 4

|PREP TIME: 10 minutes
|COOK TIME: 18 minutes

2 cups frozen waffle cut fries
2 tsps. olive oil
1 red bell pepper, chopped
2 green onions, sliced
1 cup shredded Swiss cheese
½ cup bottled chicken gravy

1. Toss the waffle fries with the olive oil.
2. Install a crisper plate in a basket. Place waffle fries in the basket, then insert basket in unit.
3. Select Zone 1, select AIR FRY, set temperature to 380°F, and set time to 18 minutes. Press the START/PAUSE button to begin cooking.
4. With 6 minutes remaining, press START/PAUSE to pause the unit. Remove the basket from unit and shake for 10 seconds. Transfer the fries to a 7 x 5-inch baking pan and top with the pepper, green onions, and cheese. Reinsert basket in unit and press START/PAUSE to resume cooking.
5. With 2 minutes remaining, press START/PAUSE to pause the unit. Remove the basket from unit and drizzle the gravy over the fries. Reinsert basket in unit and press START/PAUSE to resume cooking.
6. When cooking is complete, remove basket from unit. Serve immediately.

CHAPTER 10
Dessert

Flavor-Packed Clafoutis

|PREP TIME: 10 minutes
|COOK TIME: 25 minutes

1½ cups fresh cherries, pitted
¼ cup flour
1 egg
1 tbsp. butter
3 tbsps. vodka
2 tbsps. sugar
Pinch of salt
½ cup sour cream
¼ cup powdered sugar

1. Grease a 7 x 5-inch baking pan lightly.
2. Mix cherries and vodka in a bowl.
3. Sift together flour, sugar and salt in another bowl.
4. Stir in the sour cream and egg until a smooth dough is formed.
5. Transfer the dough evenly into the baking pan and top with the cherry mixture and butter.
6. Install a crisper plate in a basket. Place the baking pan in the basket, then insert basket in unit.
7. Select Zone 1, select BAKE, set temperature to 355°F, and set time to 25 minutes. Press the START/PAUSE button to begin cooking.
8. When cooking is complete, dust with powdered sugar and serve warm.

Shortbread Fingers

Serves: 10

|PREP TIME: 10 minutes
|COOK TIME: 14 minutes

cooking spray
1⅔ cups plain flour
¾ cup butter
⅓ cup caster sugar

1. Mix sugar, flour and butter in a bowl to form a dough.
2. Cut the dough into 10 equal sized fingers and prick the fingers lightly with a fork.
3. Install a crisper plate in both baskets and spray with cooking spray. Place 5 fingers in a single layer in each basket.
4. Select Zone 1, select BAKE, set temperature to 355°F, and set time to 14 minutes. Select MATCH COOK to match Zone 2 settings to Zone 1. Select START/PAUSE to begin cooking.
5. When cooking is complete, dish out and serve warm.

Cream Cheese Cupcakes

Serves: 10

|PREP TIME: 10 minutes
|COOK TIME: 20 minutes

cooking spray
4½-ounce self-rising flour
½-ounce cream cheese, softened
4¾-ounce butter, softened
2 eggs
½ cup fresh raspberries
Pinch of salt
4¼-ounce caster sugar
2 tsps. fresh lemon juice

1. Grease 10 silicon cups with cooking spray lightly.
2. Mix flour, baking powder and salt in a bowl.
3. Combine cream cheese, sugar, eggs and butter in another bowl.
4. Mix the flour mixture with the cream cheese mixture and squeeze in the lemon juice.
5. Transfer the mixture into 10 silicon cups and top each cup with 2 raspberries.
6. Install a crisper plate in both baskets. Place half of the silicon cups in a single layer in each basket.
7. Select Zone 1, select BAKE, set temperature to 365°F, and set time to 20 minutes. Select MATCH COOK to match Zone 2 settings to Zone 1. Select START/PAUSE to begin cooking.
8. When cooking is complete, dish out and serve to enjoy.

Buttered Dinner Rolls

Serves: 12

|PREP TIME: 15 minutes
|COOK TIME: 23 minutes

cooking spray
1 cup milk
3 cups plain flour
7½ tbsps. unsalted butter

1 tbsp. coconut oil
1 tbsp. olive oil
1 tsp. yeast
Salt and black pepper, to taste

1. Put olive oil, milk and coconut oil in a pan and cook for about 3 minutes.
2. Remove from the heat and mix well.
3. Mix together plain flour, yeast, butter, salt and black pepper in a large bowl.
4. Knead well for about 5 minutes until a dough is formed.
5. Cover the dough with a damp cloth and keep aside for about 5 minutes in a warm place.
6. Knead the dough for about 5 minutes again with your hands.
7. Cover the dough with a damp cloth and keep aside for about 30 minutes in a warm place.
8. Divide the dough into 12 equal pieces and roll each into a ball.
9. Install a crisper plate in both baskets and spray with cooking spray. Place 6 balls in a single layer in each basket.
10. Select Zone 1, select BAKE, set temperature to 360°F, and set time to 20 minutes. Select MATCH COOK to match Zone 2 settings to Zone 1. Select START/PAUSE to begin cooking.
11. When cooking is complete, transfer balls to a plate. Serve warm.

Chocolate Balls

Serves: 8

|PREP TIME: 15 minutes
|COOK TIME: 13 minutes

cooking spray
2 cups plain flour
2 tbsps. cocoa powder
¾ cup chilled butter
¼ cup chocolate, chopped into 8 chunks
½ cup icing sugar
Pinch of ground cinnamon
1 tsp. vanilla extract

1. Mix flour, icing sugar, cocoa powder, cinnamon and vanilla extract in a bowl.
2. Add cold butter and buttermilk and mix until a smooth dough is formed.
3. Divide the dough into 8 equal balls and press 1 chocolate chunk in the center of each ball. Cover completely with the dough.
4. Install a crisper plate in both baskets and spray with cooking spray. Place 4 balls in a single layer in each basket.
5. Select Zone 1, select BAKE, set temperature to 355°F, and set time to 13 minutes. Select MATCH COOK to match Zone 2 settings to Zone 1. Select START/PAUSE to begin cooking.
6. When the Zone 1 and 2 times reach 5 minutes, press START/PAUSE to pause the unit. Set the Air fryer to 320ºF and press START/PAUSE to resume cooking.
7. When cooking is complete, transfer balls to a plate. Serve warm.

Fried Golden Bananas

Serves: 6

|PREP TIME: 5 minutes
|COOK TIME: 7 minutes

1 large egg
¼ cup cornstarch
¼ cup plain bread crumbs
3 bananas, halved crosswise
Cooking oil
Chocolate sauce, for drizzling

1. In a small bowl, beat the egg. In another bowl, place the cornstarch. Put the bread crumbs in a third bowl.
2. Dip the bananas in the cornstarch, then the egg, and then the bread crumbs.
3. Install a crisper plate in a basket and spray with cooking oil. Place bananas in the basket, then insert basket in unit.
4. Select Zone 1, select AIR FRY, set temperature to 350°F, and set time to 7 minutes. Press the START/PAUSE button to begin cooking.
5. With 3 minutes remaining, press START/PAUSE to pause the unit. Remove the basket from unit and flip the bananas over. Reinsert basket in unit and press START/PAUSE to resume cooking.
6. When cooking is complete, remove basket from unit. Transfer bananas to a plate. Drizzle the chocolate sauce over the bananas, and serve.

Sweet Wontons

|PREP TIME: 15 minutes
|COOK TIME: 13 minutes

For the Wonton Wrappers:
18-ounce cream cheese, softened
1 Package of wonton wrappers
½ cup powdered sugar
1 tsp. vanilla extract
For the Raspberry Syrup:
1 (12-ounce) package frozen raspberries
¼ cup water
¼ cup sugar
1 tsp. vanilla extract

For the Wonton Wrappers:
1. Mix sugar, cream cheese and vanilla extract in a bowl and place a wonton wrapper on a work surface.
2. Place about 1 tbsp. of the cream cheese mixture in the center of each wonton wrapper.
3. Fold the wrappers around the filling and seal the edges.
4. Install a crisper plate in a basket. Place wontons in the basket, then insert basket in unit.
5. Select Zone 1, select AIR FRY, set temperature to 350°F, and set time to 8 minutes. Press the START/PAUSE button to begin cooking.
6. When cooking is complete, remove basket from unit. Transfer wontons to a plate.
For the Raspberry Syrup:
7. Put water, sugar, raspberries and vanilla in a skillet on medium heat and cook for about 5 minutes, stirring continuously.
8. Transfer the mixture into the food processor and blend until smooth.
9. Drizzle the raspberry syrup over the wontons to serve.

Cheesy Dinner Rolls

|PREP TIME: 10 minutes
|COOK TIME: 6 minutes

Cooking spray
2 dinner rolls
½ cup Parmesan cheese, grated
2 tbsps. unsalted butter, melted
½ tsp. garlic bread seasoning mix

1. Cut the dinner rolls in slits and stuff cheese in the slits.
2. Top with butter and garlic bread seasoning mix.
3. Install a crisper plate in a basket and spray with cooking spray. Place dinner rolls in the basket, then insert basket in unit.
4. Select Zone 1, select BAKE, set temperature to 355°F, and set time to 6 minutes. Press the START/PAUSE button to begin cooking.
5. With 3 minutes remaining, press START/PAUSE to pause the unit. Remove the basket from unit and flip the dinner rolls over. Reinsert basket in unit and press START/PAUSE to resume cooking.
6. When cooking is complete, remove basket from unit. Transfer dinner rolls to a plate. Serve warm.

Basic Butter Cookies

Serves: 8

|PREP TIME: 10 minutes
|COOK TIME: 10 minutes

4-ounce unsalted butter
1 cup all-purpose flour
¼ tsp. baking powder
1¼-ounce icing sugar

1. Grease a 7 x 5-inch baking dish lightly.
2. Mix butter, icing sugar, flour and baking powder in a large bowl.
3. Mix well until a dough is formed and transfer into the piping bag fitted with a fluted nozzle. Pipe the dough onto the baking dish.
4. Install a crisper plate in a basket. Place baking dish in the basket, then insert basket in unit.
5. Select Zone 1, select BAKE, set temperature to 340°F, and set time to 10 minutes. Press the START/PAUSE button to begin cooking, until golden brown.
6. When cooking is complete, serve warm.

Double Chocolate Muffins

Serves: 12

|PREP TIME: 20 minutes
|COOK TIME: 30 minutes

1⅓ cups self-rising flour
2½ tbsps. cocoa powder
3½ ounces butter
5 tbsps. milk
2½ ounces milk chocolate, finely chopped
⅔ cup plus 3 tbsps. caster sugar
½ tsp. vanilla extract

1. Grease 12 muffin molds lightly.
2. Mix flour, sugar, and cocoa powder in a bowl.
3. Stir in the butter, milk, vanilla extract and the chopped chocolate and mix until well combined. Transfer the mixture evenly into the muffin molds.
4. Install a crisper plate in both baskets. Place half of the muffin molds in each basket.
5. Select Zone 1, select BAKE, set temperature to 355°F, and set time to 16 minutes. Select MATCH COOK to match Zone 2 settings to Zone 1. Select START/PAUSE to begin cooking.
6. When the Zone 1 and 2 times reach 6 minutes, press START/PAUSE to pause the unit. Set the Air fryer to 320ºF and press START/PAUSE to resume cooking.
7. When cooking is complete, serve warm.

Chocolate Yogurt Pecans Muffins

PREP TIME: 15 minutes
COOK TIME: 12 minutes

1½ cups all-purpose flour
2 tsps. baking powder
1 cup yogurt
¼ cup mini chocolate chips
¼ cup pecans, chopped
¼ cup sugar
½ tsp. salt
⅓ cup vegetable oil
2 tsps. vanilla extract

1. Grease 8 muffin molds lightly.
2. Mix flour, sugar, baking powder, and salt in a bowl.
3. Mix the yogurt, oil, and vanilla extract in another bowl.
4. Fold in the chocolate chips and pecans and divide the mixture evenly into the muffin molds.
5. Install a crisper plate in both baskets. Place 4 muffin molds in a single layer in each basket.
6. Select Zone 1, select BAKE, set temperature to 355°F, and set time to 12 minutes. Select MATCH COOK to match Zone 2 settings to Zone 1. Select START/PAUSE to begin cooking.
7. When cooking is complete, remove the muffin molds from Air fryer and invert the muffins onto wire rack to cool completely before serving.

Citric Chocolate Pudding

PREP TIME: 10 minutes
COOK TIME: 12 minutes

½ cup butter
⅔ cup dark chocolate, chopped
2 medium eggs
2 tsps. fresh orange rind, grated finely
2 tbsps. self-rising flour
¼ cup caster sugar
¼ cup fresh orange juice

1. Grease four 3-inch ramekins lightly.
2. Microwave butter and chocolate in a bowl on high for about 2 minutes.
3. Add sugar, eggs, orange rind and juice and mix until well combined.
4. Stir in the flour and mix well. Divide this mixture into the ramekins.
5. Install a crisper plate in both baskets. Place 2 ramekins in each basket.
6. Select Zone 1, select BAKE, set temperature to 355°F, and set time to 12 minutes. Select MATCH COOK to match Zone 2 settings to Zone 1. Select START/PAUSE to begin cooking.
7. When cooking is complete, dish out and serve chilled.

Appendix 1: Basic Kitchen Conversions & Equivalents

DRY MEASUREMENTS CONVERSION CHART

3 teaspoons = 1 tablespoon = 1/16 cup
6 teaspoons = 2 tablespoons = 1/8 cup
12 teaspoons = 4 tablespoons = ¼ cup
24 teaspoons = 8 tablespoons = ½ cup
36 teaspoons = 12 tablespoons = ¾ cup
48 teaspoons = 16 tablespoons = 1 cup

METRIC TO US COOKING CONVERSIONS

OVEN TEMPERATURES

120 ºC = 250 ºF
160 ºC = 320 ºF
180 ºC = 350 ºF
205 ºC = 400 ºF
220 ºC = 425 ºF

LIQUID MEASUREMENTS CONVERSION CHART

8 fluid ounces = 1 cup = ½ pint = ¼ quart
16 fluid ounces = 2 cups = 1 pint = ½ quart
32 fluid ounces = 4 cups = 2 pints = 1 quart = ¼ gallon
128 fluid ounces = 16 cups = 8 pints = 4 quarts = 1 gallon

BAKING IN GRAMS

1 cup flour = 140 grams
1 cup sugar = 150 grams
1 cup powdered sugar = 160 grams
1 cup heavy cream = 235 grams

VOLUME

1 milliliter = 1/5 teaspoon
5 ml = 1 teaspoon
15 ml = 1 tablespoon
240 ml = 1 cup or 8 fluid ounces
1 liter = 34 fluid ounces

WEIGHT

1 gram = .035 ounces
100 grams = 3.5 ounces
500 grams = 1.1 pounds
1 kilogram = 35 ounces

US TO METRIC COOKING CONVERSIONS

1/5 tsp = 1 ml
1 tsp = 5 ml
1 tbsp = 15 ml
1 fluid ounces = 30 ml
1 cup = 237 ml
1 pint (2 cups) = 473 ml
1 quart (4 cups) = .95 liter
1 gallon (16 cups) = 3.8 liters
1 oz = 28 grams
1 pound = 454 grams

BUTTER

1 cup butter = 2 sticks = 8 ounces = 230 grams
= 16 tablespoons

WHAT DOES 1 CUP EQUAL

1 cup = 8 fluid ounces
1 cup = 16 tablespoons
1 cup = 48 teaspoons
1 cup = ½ pint
1 cup = ¼ quart
1 cup = 1/16 gallon
1 cup = 240 ml

BAKING PAN CONVERSIONS

9-inch round cake pan = 12 cups
10-inch tube pan =16 cups
10-inch bundt pan = 12 cups
9-inch springform pan = 10 cups
9 x 5 inch loaf pan = 8 cups
9-inch square pan = 8 cups

BAKING PAN CONVERSIONS

1 cup all-purpose flour = 4.5 oz
1 cup rolled oats = 3 oz
1 large egg = 1.7 oz
1 cup butter = 8 oz
1 cup milk = 8 oz
1 cup heavy cream = 8.4 oz
1 cup granulated sugar = 7.1 oz
1 cup packed brown sugar = 7.75 oz
1 cup vegetable oil = 7.7 oz
1 cup unsifted powdered sugar = 4.4 oz

Appendix 2: Recipes Index

Made in the USA
Columbia, SC
29 November 2024